SACRAMENTO PUBLIC LIBRARY

SACRAMENTO PUBLIC LIBRARY
828 "I" STREET
SACRAMENTO, CA 95814
1/2013

3 3029 00597 2781

CEN B Stalin
1
Rigby, Thom Stalin, edited by T
N. J., Prentice-Hall 1966
3 3029 00597 2781

B
Stalin
Rigby
Stalin 76   495

c.1

D0500315

CENTRAL
SACRAMENTO CITY-COUNTY LIBRARY
SACRAMENTO, CALIFORNIA

GREAT LIVES OBSERVED

Gerald Emanuel Stearn, *General Editor*

EACH VOLUME IN THE SERIES VIEWS THE CHARACTER AND ACHIEVE-
MENT OF A GREAT WORLD FIGURE IN THREE PERSPECTIVES—
THROUGH HIS OWN WORDS, THROUGH THE OPINIONS OF HIS CON-
TEMPORARIES, AND THROUGH RETROSPECTIVE JUDGMENTS—THUS
COMBINING THE INTIMACY OF AUTOBIOGRAPHY, THE IMMEDIACY
OF EYE-WITNESS OBSERVATION, AND THE COMPARATIVE OBJECTIVITY
OF MODERN SCHOLARSHIP.

T. H. RIGBY, *the editor of this volume, is Professorial Fellow
in Political Science at the Institute of Advanced Studies, Aus-
tralian National University. He has served as Secretary to the
British Embassy in Moscow and as Visiting Professor at the
Russian Institute of Columbia University. The author of numerous articles on Soviet government and politics, he is also
co-editor of* The Disintegrating Monolith: Pluralist Trends in
International Communism.

Forthcoming volumes in the Great Lives Observed series

Hitler, *edited by George Stein*

Jesus, *edited by Hugh Anderson*

Lincoln, *edited by James Shenton*

Luther, *edited by Paul Lee*

Franklin Delano Roosevelt, *edited by Gerald Nash*

GREAT LIVES OBSERVED

Stalin

Edited by T. H. RIGBY

*The vengeance of history is
more terrible than the
vengeance of the most powerful
General Secretary.*

—TROTSKY

A SPECTRUM BOOK

PRENTICE-HALL, INC., ENGLEWOOD CLIFFS, N.J.

79 Encyc Brit. Indepth

B

Stalin

Copyright © 1966 by PRENTICE-HALL, INC.,
Englewood Cliffs, New Jersey.
A SPECTRUM BOOK

All rights reserved.
No part of this book may be reproduced
in any form, by mimeograph or any other means,
without permission in writing from the publishers.

Current printing (last number):

10 9 8 7 6 5 4 3 2 1

Library of Congress Catalog Card Number 66-16348

Printed in the United States of America—C

P84045, C84046

NOV 8 1966

Contents

c. 1

PART ONE

STALIN LOOKS AT THE WORLD

1

The Era of Imperialism and the Proletarian Revolution, *24*   The Dictatorship of the Proletariat, *27*   The Peasant and National Problems, *29*   Strategy and Tactics, *31*   The Party, *32*   Style in Work, *35*

2

Why I Became a Revolutionary, *37*   My Revolutionary Apprenticeship, *38*   A Lenin Literary, *40*   How to Deal With Opposition, *41*   The Future Communist Society, *43*   The State Under Communism, *44*   Creating the New Class, *45*   The Socialist Fatherland, *47*   Stalin As War Leader, *48*   Stalinism As Usual, *52*   Basis and Superstructure, *53*

3

The Will to Transform, *58*   The Cult of Necessity, *60*   The Formula for Man, *64*

v

THE CITY LIBRARY
SACRAMENTO, CALIF.

GREAT LIVES OBSERVED

STALIN

Introduction

The first half of the twentieth century was one of those climacteric periods in human history when long-established patterns began to break up and secular trends were halted or reversed. An era of relative peace and civilized international order expired in two world wars of unprecedented scale and destructiveness. Belief in the irresistible spread of freedom and reason was shattered, new forms of tyranny arose, and men enslaved themselves to mass movements, ideologies, and leaders. The dominance of Asia and Africa by a handful of European nations reached its apogee, was challenged, and began to collapse. This was an intensely political era, when the momentum in human affairs shifted from the spheres of ideas and economics to the sphere of the dominance over and manipulation of men. It was an era of "movement regimes," [1] of dictators backed by movements dedicated to the salvation or remaking of national or international society: of Atatürks, Lenins, Mussolinis, Hitlers, and Francos, of Titos, Ho Chi-minhs, Perons, and Stalins.

No man more fully epitomized this era than did Josif Stalin. His political career was channeled through the type-case of twentieth-century political movements, and coincided almost exactly with the first half of the century. He became the twentieth-century dictator *par excellence,* exercising power over more men and for a longer period than any of his fellow dictators. The movement he dominated was world-wide in its extent and ambitions, unlimited in its revolutionary scope. A semi-European who gained power over an ideology and a movement deeply rooted in European civilization, he employed that power not only to attack Europe's international political position but also to culturally de-Europeanize his own domains. Under his influence the ideology itself was deprived of its rational and liberalizing core and refashioned into an incantatory cult and a rationalization of tyranny.

Stalin's career also epitomized the central role of political power which characterized his era. It was not merely that his regime

---

[1] The concept is Robert C. Tucker's. See his "Towards a Comparative Study of Movement Regimes," *American Political Science Review* (June 1961), reprinted in *The Soviet Political Mind* (New York and London, 1963).

1

rested heavily on the use of force, fear, and falsehood. Though Stalin understood the potency of ideological and economic factors, he never allowed them to take precedence over political considerations: he invariably translated them into political terms. He enjoyed a superb capacity for manipulating men and institutions so as to enhance his own influence and control. At the height of his power Stalin was invested with the synthetic charisma of a "beloved father and teacher" and "savior of the Soviet peoples." He was acknowledged as the foremost interpreter of Marxism and Leninism, and, during World War II, he became a bemedaled generalissimo. But the qualities which won him power were not those of the charismatic prophet or leader, the party theoretician, or the military hero, but rather those of the brilliant politician. This fact is not always grasped in Western countries, where "politics" means such things as a party system, competitive elections, association for the furtherance of group interests, and open debate of public issues. Most social structures provide scope for that peculiar combination of qualities characteristic of the successful politician: (a) great reserves of energy; (b) persistence and resilience; (c) awareness of when to assert one's will and (d) when to compromise; (e) ability to form and change tactical alliances untrammeled by sentiment; (f) strength to isolate one's rivals; (g) courage and willingness to take risks; (h) capacity for mastering and memorizing detail while arriving quickly at the essentials of a problem; (i) sensitivity to the drift of events and of social moods and processes; and (j) judgment in choosing which of these to obstruct and which to adopt and promote. The student of Stalin will readily recognize here the very qualities by which he won and held power. If politics is the art of the possible, then Stalin mastered this in the highest degree, and he mastered both aspects of it: the negative aspect of recognizing the limits beyond which particular objectives may not be profitably or safely pressed, and the positive aspect of perceiving the opportunities presented by a given situation, if properly exploited.

Stalin, then, was not merely a dominant figure of his era: he *represented* it, in the sense that his personality and his career manifested some of its most distinctive features in highly concentrated form. In view of this, it may seem strange that more than a decade was to pass after his death without a single full-length, scholarly biography appearing in any language. In large part the explanation lies in both the achievements and the limitations of what was written about Stalin during his lifetime.

This writing[2] proceeded on a number of distinct levels. There were, firstly, the official biographies. Never very informative, these quickly acquired the character of standardized panegyric. The same quality attached to incidental discussions of Stalin's activities, ideas, and personality in Soviet writings on history, politics, and Marxist theory from the late 1920s on.

Secondly, there were memoirs written abroad by Soviet émigrés or defectors, claiming to have known Stalin in his youth, to have come in contact with him in the course of their official duties, or to have had access to information about him through friends in his entourage. Unfortunately, while this material has yielded scraps of valuable information, it has for the most part proved either spurious or such a mélange of fact and imaginative reconstruction that historians have been able to make little use of it. This is particularly regrettable so far as memoirs regarding Stalin's early years in the Caucasus are concerned, in view of the paucity of other sources on this, the formative period of his life. It is also a matter for regret that the greatest of all refugees from Stalinism, Trotsky, did not include in his voluminous writings on Stalin and Stalin's Russia a simple, circumstantial record of his own observations of Stalin in action.

Next, there were the reports of foreign journalists, statesmen, and diplomats who interviewed Stalin or had dealings with him. These varied from the acutely perceptive (e.g., Hilger, Churchill) to the naïve or uncomprehending (e.g., Ludwig, Davies). Taken together they constitute an invaluable and essential source for the study of Stalin's personality and his impact on his time.

Stalin was inevitably the subject of innumerable popular, commercial biographies, of which the classic was Essad-Bey's *Stalin, the Career of a Fanatic,* originally published in Germany in 1931. The remoteness and mysteriousness of the man and his setting as well as the esoteric character of the original sources subjected the commercial biographer to the seemingly irresistible temptation of embellishing history with anecdote, romanticizing the narrative, or providing it with a fanciful psychological or ethnological framework.

Three works—those of Trotsky, Souvarine, and Deutscher—may be regarded as the classical biographies of Stalin. While the first two stopped with the great purges, and Deutscher's account was written from the perspective of the postwar years, these works

[2] Full details of the works referred to in this section are given in the Bibliographical Note.

nevertheless have much in common. All are intensely political. They concentrate heavily on Stalin's political career and significance while touching little on his personal and inner life. All combine literary brilliance with a firm factual basis, although Souvarine was less accurate in detail than the other two. These writers shared a common background in the communist movement, both Souvarine and Deutscher having been Trotskyites in their time, the first in France and the second in Poland. Furthermore, their intellectual orientations remained sufficiently alike for them all to recur to the French Revolution as a framework of reference and to link Stalin as a political phenomenon with the attempt to impose socialism on a society unready for it. They diverged sharply, however, in their evaluation of this link. For Souvarine and Trotsky, Stalin was a mediocrity with a lust for power: he betrayed the revolution; for Deutscher he was a tyrant who perpetrated great horrors, but whose *virtu* nevertheless ensured that the foundations of socialism were built and successfully defended, despite the most adverse circumstances.

Certain conclusions emerge from this brief survey of the literature about Stalin up to his death. First, the sharp limitations to what could be said about his early years, his personal life, and his psyche had been made abundantly clear. Second, those aspects where factual data was relatively abundant, particularly the political history of the Civil War and the 1920s, had been closely studied by first-class minds, whose main findings were widely known. Third, so far as interpretation was concerned, all the changes—Marxian, Freudian, ethnological, and what have you—had already been rung. This helps to explain why the years since Stalin's death have not produced the crop of major biographical studies that might have been expected on the death of such a mighty ruler. The scholarly course appeared to be to hold one's peace, pending the uncovering of important new data.

It would be wrong to conclude, however, that the years since 1953 have contributed nothing to our understanding of Stalin. Some new information has emerged, most dramatically in Khrushchev's speeches to the Twentieth and Twenty-second Congresses of the Soviet Communist Party and in Milovan Djilas's *Conversations With Stalin*. Isolated facts, mentioned in Soviet publications since 1962 in the course of historical or other articles (obituaries, memoirs), are of great interest. Some light has also been thrown on the political history of Stalin's last years by "kremlinological" research aimed largely at elucidating past relationships among the Soviet leaders with a view to following intelligently the politics of the succession to Stalin. Finally, the changes in Soviet society since 1953 have provoked renewed consideration by historians and political scientists of the part played in the evolution of the Soviet system by Marxism, by Russian history and traditions, and by the accidents of personality. For some years an intermittent controversy has been carried on along these lines, mainly in magazines of opinion and scholarly journals. Much of this discussion has centered on the nature and sources of "Stalinism" and whether or not it was "inevitable." The new facts and perspectives acquired since 1953 have significantly affected the picture of Stalin which emerges from such recent historical works as Schapiro's *The Communist Party of the Soviet Union* and Armstrong's *The Politics of Totalitarianism*.

The second half of the 1960s will probably witness a major reappraisal of Stalin and the Stalin era. This task is indeed already engaging the attentions of a number of Western scholars, whose efforts have good prospects of being nourished by increasingly objective and informative treatment of Stalin in the Soviet Union itself. This book aims at contributing to the enterprise of reappraisal first by presenting the reader with an immediate impression of Stalin, both through his own words uttered or written in various moods and circumstances, and through the first-hand evaluations of men who spoke and dealt with him, and then by introducing the reader to major interpretations of his character, achievements, and place in history. As an aid to evaluating Stalin's impact on the Soviet mind and emotions, material is included illustrative of the Stalin cult as well as of the nature and extent of its subsequent repudiation.

To orient the student in using this material, it will first be desirable to set out briefly the principal known facts about Stalin's background, life and political career. While every effort will be made to present this account in an objective and dispassionate manner, a reminder should, perhaps, be given of the editor's particular point of view, which sees Stalin above all as a brilliant (if ruthless) politician operating in an intensely political age, a point of view which would not command universal assent. The student will have the opportunity of judging the efficacy of this point of view when he considers the varied evidence and evaluations assembled in later sections of the book. Meanwhile the biographical sketch that follows, as well as providing a framework of reference for the readings, should help to clarify the editor's evaluation and to indicate why Stalin's political talents were deployed in the particular way they were.

We have referred to Stalin as a semi-European. Transcaucasia, where Stalin spent his childhood and youth, lay on the fringes of the Russian Empire, just as Russia itself lay on the fringes of Europe.

For generations scholars have debated whether Russia is "really" part of Europe. In large part the debate is a semantic one, and it is more instructive to ask *in what respects* Russia resembled other parts of Europe and in what respects it differed. Quite close ethnic links and a shared heritage of Christianity constitute important common ground between the Russians and the peoples of Central and Western Europe. On the other hand, Russia was by-passed by a number of experiences of vital importance in forming the nations of the West: the religious, legal, and intellectual traditions of the Roman Church, the intricate medieval socio-political pattern of feudal class, chartered towns, and clergy, the renaissance and reformation, and the maritime discovery of the non-European world. Instead, she was heir to the spiritual and political traditions of Byzantium and languished for generations under the Mongol yoke. A powerful centralized monarchy emerged in Russia at much the same time as in Western Europe, but whereas in the latter its emergence was associated with the decline of the serf-owning nobility and the rise of the towns, in Russia it was associated with the *creation* of serfdom and of a new serf-owning nobility owing service to the state. By the seventeenth century Russia had grown very remote, socially, politically, and culturally, from the nations of the Atlantic seaboard.

The reforms of Peter the Great (1672-1725), who sought to modernize his country by wholesale and harshly imposed imitation of the West, created an up-to-date bureaucracy and military establishment staffed by a nobility Western in dress, manners, and education, but made little impact on the townsmen, the clergy, and the peasantry, who formed the overwhelming bulk of the population. While Westernization made possible the brilliant cultural achievements of nineteenth-century Russia, it also opened up a profound cleavage in Russian society and culture. That unique phenomenon, the Russian intelligentsia, may have been begotten by the Enlightenment, but it was this schizophrenic society and culture which gave it birth. The Russian *intelligent*, fascinated on the one hand by "Europe" and on the other by "the people," and avid to bridge the gulf between them, was driven on the one side to high intellectual achievement and moral heroism, and on the other to deeds of violence and destruction. With a rare intensity he seized on every current of Western philosophical, social, and political theory. Then he generated new theories of his own and developed traditions of clandestine organization for purposes of revolutionary propaganda and action.

In the 1860s the Tsarist autocracy, weakened by the Crimean War, yielded to its critics and abolished serfdom, introduced certain legal safeguards for the citizen, and provided for elective councils to participate in limited aspects of provincial and local government. The peasants, however, did not become independent proprietors, and felt cheated by the terms of their emancipation. Political opposition was renewed and an atmosphere of bitterness was engendered which drove the regime and its critics in an ascending spiral of repression and violence. Meanwhile the beginnings of industrialization, accelerating rapidly from the 1880s, were creating in Russia a proletariat fitting ominously the classic *Communist Manifesto* formulae of Marx and Engels, living and working in appalling conditions, with "nothing but their chains to lose"; a proletariat, moreover, drawn from the villages and preserving close links with the villages, so that their proletarian resentments were thereby reinforced by the resentments of a land-hungry peasantry. A section of the revolutionary intelligentsia now turned to Marxism, seeing in the proletariat the means of overturning the autocracy and ending the backwardness and oppressiveness of Russian life. Clandestine Marxist circles emerged in the 1880s, and gained strength from a series of massive strikes in the mid-nineties. In 1898 a number of their representatives met secretly in Minsk and formed The Russian Social-Democratic Worker's Party (RSDWP).

It is all too easy to oversimplify the problem of Russia and Europe by tacitly identifying Europe with the Atlantic seaboard or "the West" and forgetting how recently the West acquired many of its salient features. Most of the "distinctive" elements of Tsarist Russia—such as the autocratic government and lack of representative institutions; the sharp distinction of society into "estates"; the persistence of serfdom; the omnipresent bureaucracy; censorship, and political police—can be matched in wide areas of continental Europe during the eighteenth and nineteenth centuries. Yet, as one moved from west to east across the continent, such elements did become more marked and did prove more resistant to change; moreover in Russia both they and the public reaction to them were strongly colored by those peculiarities of the country's historical development that we have already noted.

In its efforts to safeguard its frontiers and to open up new land for settlement, Tsarist Russia continuously expanded its territories from the sixteenth century on until it contained as many non-Russians as Russians. Illegal nationalist movements emerged among many of these subject peoples during the nineteenth century, and national resentments also made them fertile recruiting grounds for the major revolutionary parties of the Empire.

The Caucasus was the Balkans of the Russian Empire: it had the same hodgepodge of ardently xenophobic peoples, the same blend of Byzantine Christian and Turco-Arab culture, the same backward, dependent peasantry and fiercely independent mountaineers.

Vissarion Djugashvili was a rather enterprising, though otherwise typical, son of the Tsar's Caucasian "Balkans": an ex-serf from the Georgian mountain village of Didi-Lilo who sought in vain to establish himself as a shoemaker in the district center of Gori. Having failed at this, he joined the sweated labor in a Tiflis shoe factory. Djugashvili's young wife bore (and lost) three babies before giving birth to the one, christened Josif, who survived. His earnings insufficient to support his small family and his wife forced to slave as a washerwoman, Djugashvili became embittered. It is said he found release in vodka and harsh beatings of his young son.[3] He died when Josif was eleven years old.

It was Josif's mother who was the central factor in his young life, who cherished for him dreams of a prestige career as a priest, and who saved and scraped to keep him at the Gori church school, where at the age of fifteen his successes won him a place in the Tiflis Theological Seminary. The Seminary, though joyless, obscurantist, and harshly disciplined, was regarded as the major educational establishment of the Caucasus; it was also known as a hotbed of clandestine nationalism and radicalism, which the administration met with harsh punishments and expulsions. There is no need, therefore, to invoke any exceptional virtues or defects of character to explain why the young seminarist Djugashvili soon

[3] Stalin's biographers differ in their evaluation of reports of Vissarion Djugashvili's drunkenness and ill-treatment of his son. Some have seen here the clue to Stalin's vengeful, rebellious, and devious character. Cf. Leon Trotsky, *Stalin, An Appraisal of the Man and His Influence* (New York, 1941; London, 1947), pp. 7-8; Isaac Deutscher, *Stalin: A Political Biography* (New York and London, 1949), pp. 3-4.

became involved with political opposition. In his third year he was being punished for reading forbidden books, in his fourth year he joined a clandestine Social-Democratic group in Tiflis known as Messame Dassy. He was soon conducting socialist study groups of factory workers, and, in his fifth year, he was expelled from the seminary. (Although political factors certainly lay behind his expulsion, how directly they were responsible is not clear.)

The eighteen-year-old Djugashvili's involvement with the illegal socialist movement grew in the months of unemployment that followed his removal from the seminary. For a time he took work as a clerk in the Tiflis Observatory, but this came to an end when the police searched his room. So began Josif's career in the revolutionary underground, a life of dedicated privation, of living under a succession of aliases subject to constant threat of arrest, of clandestine meetings and clandestine correspondence, of organizing and conducting study circles and demonstrations, of composing leaflets and articles for illegal publications—a constant testing of wit and will against both the Tsarist political police and rival groupings within the opposition. He soon began to make his mark. In 1901, two years after leaving the seminary, his first articles began to appear in the illegal Georgian socialist periodical *Brdzola,* he was elected to the nine-man Tiflis Social-Democratic Committee, whose sphere of influence covered the whole Caucasus, and he was sent as party organizer to the oil port of Batum. Here, adopting the nickname "Koba," [4] he succeeded in establishing a secret press by which he stirred the workers to violent action. In April 1902 he was arrested for the first time, and remained in various Georgian prisons until November 1903, when he was deported to Siberia. Within a month, however, he escaped from his place of exile, and by the outbreak of the Russo-Japanese War in February 1904 was back in Tiflis.

One feature stands out in this first phase of Djugashvili-Koba's revolutionary career: he was a radical, a "hard." In each of the major struggles over Marxist theory and policy which wracked the infant Russian Social-Democratic movement, it was the more political, the more revolutionary, the tougher line that Djugashvili followed. Thus he joined with the supporters of illegal, political action, in opposition to the "Legal Marxists" and the "Economists."

[4] In keeping with his clandestine roles, Josif Vissarionovitch became "Koba" (The Indomitable), "Ivanovich," "Gayoz Nisharodze," "K. Cato," among others. By 1912, he was signing articles "K. Stalin." Soviet publications cite him as "J. V. Stalin."

When Lenin and his friends sought to weld the various local Social-Democratic groups and committees into a coherent, centralized organization, through the distribution-network of the illegal periodical *Iskra,* Djugashvili was quick to identify himself as an *Iskra* man. He seems to have been too radical for the leader of the Tiflis Committee, Djibladze, who was probably glad to pack him off to Batum (although friction on a more personal level may have been a factor here too). Similarly, in Batum he aroused the alarm and hostility of local socialist leaders, who feared that his forceful tactics might wreck all their careful, preparatory work.

Meanwhile, there were momentous developments in the émigré leadership of the party. In 1902 Lenin published his pamphlet *What is to be Done,* in which he set out his blueprint for the party as a highly disciplined, centralized conspiratorial organization of professional revolutionaries, not merged with the working-class movement, but directing and coordinating it in the interests of the Revolution. Lenin's concept of revolutionary organization and of the proper relationship between the revolutionary party and the masses continued a well-established tradition of the Russian revolutionary intelligentsia, but it was deeply repugnant to the democratic beliefs and sentiments which had long been an integral part of the Marxist movement. Even Lenin's principal collaborators on *Iskra* now found they could no longer go along with him. Differences came to a head at the Second Congress of the RSDWP held in Brussels and London in 1903, at which the party split into rival wings, the Bolsheviks (from *bol'she,* more), the followers of Lenin, and Mensheviks (from *men'she,* less), his opponents. All attempts to reunite the party foundered on the rock of Lenin's "ultra-centralism" or on related issues of organization or revolutionary theory and tactics.

By the time Stalin returned from his Siberian exile, the split in the émigré leadership was producing strong if confused repercussions in the local organizations. There could be little doubt which side Koba would choose. His article "The Class of Proletarians and the Party of Proletarians," written toward the end of 1904, presented a crude but forceful statement of Lenin's organizational philosophy. As the majority of Transcaucasian socialists opted for Menshevism, Stalin now became one of the leaders of a radical segment in an otherwise "moderate" organization. As several writers have pointed out, it was not only because he was a "hard" that Stalin gravitated to Bolshevism; in a movement which traditionally valued above all intellectual brilliance and mastery of the written and spoken word, which Stalin lacked, Lenin alone gave central importance to the disciplined, underground organization-man—a role for which Stalin was ideally suited.

The defeats and disorganization suffered in the Russo-Japanese War weakened the Tsarist government, and there ensued that chaos of demonstrations, strikes, mutinies, shootings, and local risings that became known as the 1905 Revolution, from which the regime extricated itself by granting certain constitutional concessions, notably the establishment of an elective parliament (the Duma). In 1907, however, by which time the Revolution had run its course, the government dispersed the Duma, arrested the socialist deputies, and unconstitutionally amended the electoral law so as to ensure a permanent right-wing majority. The left-wing parties, which had functioned relatively freely and in the open for some two years, were again forced underground and subjected to relentless and arbitrary police repression.

At the height of the Revolution, Lenin had ordered the secret establishment and arming of Bolshevik combat squads, and in some areas, notably the Caucasus, these squads continued to be active long after the Revolution subsided, their "expropriations" often degenerating into virtual banditry. It is undoubtedly significant that Stalin was one of the principal local leaders involved in master-minding the organization and exploits of these squads. By concentrating on his clandestine Mafia-like activities, however, some writers have missed his no less important achievements on a more public level during this period.

Already while in prison Stalin had been made a member of the Transcaucasian Social-Democratic Committee; the years 1905 to 1907 saw him as joint editor of a new Bolshevik newspaper in Tiflis, organizing a Caucasus-wide conference of Bolsheviks, attending the Tammerfors Bolshevik Conference as the only Caucasian delegate, participating in negotiations with the Menshevik leaders in Saint Petersburg, and attending the Fourth and Fifth Congresses of the Russian Social-Democratic Party in Stockholm and London respectively, where he was the only Bolshevik delegate from the Caucasus.

At the age of 26, Stalin now advanced into the fringe of the national leadership of Lenin's wing of the party. In 1907 he moved his center of activities from Tiflis to Baku, where the crudely exploited oil-workers provided the Bolsheviks with their main basis of proletarian support in the Caucasus. In protracted negotiations between the oil-workers' union and the employers for a collective agreement, Stalin and his comrades on the Baku Committee succeeded in keeping alive mass militancy and something of the spirit of the Revolution long after it had subsided in the country at large. In the middle of 1908, however, the Okhrana struck, and Stalin was imprisoned for some months and then deported to northern Russia. Again his exile proved short-lived; he escaped after four months, and returned for another brief period to the Baku underground before again being arrested in March 1910.

In this period, when the Russian Social-Democrats, despite a formal merger between their Bolshevik and Menshevik wings, were torn by sharp tactical disputes, Stalin appears to have stuck by and large to the Leninist line that the party must fully exploit its opportunities of both legal *and* illegal work, against those who advocated, in effect, that one or the other should be scrapped. At the same time the Baku Committee, of which he was a member, adopted a position critical of the whole émigré leadership, including Lenin, for splitting the party over theoretical "trifles" and for its incompetence in leading the underground.

The years 1910 to 1913, years of intensive bursts of activity alternating with spells in prison and banishment in northern Russia, saw Stalin move from the fringe to the inner circle of the Bolshevik leadership. The way had been opened up for him by Lenin's quarrels with some of the older leaders and the arrest of others. It was then, too, that he assumed the name of Stalin (Man of Steel). In 1912 Lenin decided on a definite break with his Menshevik and other critics. He called a conference in Prague which elected a new Central Committee of his own followers. The tough, resourceful member of the Baku Committee was now the sort of man he needed. Stalin failed to gain election to the Central Committee, but Lenin exercised his right to have him co-opted to it. Lenin also created a new Russian Bureau to direct the work of the underground, three of whose four members, including Stalin, were drawn from the Baku Committee. Further, Stalin was put in charge of the new Bolshevik daily, *Pravda,* although here, interestingly enough, he proved too conciliatory toward the Mensheviks for Lenin's taste, and he was removed. Finally, at Lenin's suggestion and under his supervision, he made his first venture into original theoretical writing, with a study of "the national question."

Stalin did not enjoy his new role for long, however. His arrest in 1913 was followed by banishment to a remote corner of Siberia where escape was virtually impossible, and whence he was only released by the 1917 Revolution. Thus his career in the revolutionary underground ended. We have already noted one characteristic of Stalin the revolutionary: his toughness, his readiness for bold, resolute action. This, however, was qualified by a willingness to compromise for the sake of shared, immediate objectives, as well as by an ability to bide his time and avoid showing his hand when the most profitable course of action was not immediately clear. A further characteristic was his impatience with theoretical discussion and his highly pragmatic attitude toward ideas. Critics have attributed a further trait to Stalin the revolutionary: a tendency to vindictiveness and intrigue in his relations within the party, and a trick of punishing those who crossed him by slyly setting others against them.[5] Such allegations are difficult to evaluate, but by 1917 his reputation in the Bolshevik underground for "certain personal traits" was bad enough to prevent his co-option as a voting member of the Central Committee Bureau (see below, chap. 4, "Certain Personal Traits").

Like the Revolution of 1905, the February 1917 Revolution was spontaneous and unplanned, catching the revolutionary parties off-guard. The Tsarist regime was replaced by a Provisional Government composed mainly of middle-class liberals. At the same time soviets (councils) of the revolutionary workers and soldiers were formed, and such was the authority of the Petrograd Soviet among the populace that it enjoyed virtually a veto-power over the decisions of the Provisional Government.

In the weeks between the outbreak of the Revolution and Lenin's arrival at Petrograd in the famous sealed train, the Bolshevik leadership was in a state of confusion. For over a decade Lenin had been talking of a Bolshevik-led alliance of workers and peasants for the overthrow of Tsarism and the introduction of a democratic capitalist order. This objective was clearly out of date, but what should replace it? Lenin now electrified his followers by calling for the replacement of the "parliamentary republic" by a Bolshevik-led "republic of soviets" which would go on to initiate a socialist program. Lenin called on all his reserves of will, resource, and persuasion to convince his party of the correctness of this course, to keep their eye on the goal in the stormy and chaotic months ahead, and finally to steel them to the task of taking power. Success was due above all to two factors: the Bolshevik slogans of immediate peace and distribution of land to the peasants, which won them the support of the revolutionary masses and eventually a majority in

[5] See Boris Souvarine, *Stalin, A Critical Survey of Bolshevism* (New York, 1939), pp. 38, 99-102; Trotsky, *op. cit.*, pp. 54, 117-21; cf. Deutscher, *op. cit.*, p. 50.

the soviets, and the successful establishment of Red Guard detachments in the factories and their superb deployment in the actual seizure of power.[6] The first they owed to Lenin, the second to Lenin's former critic and new-won ally, Trotsky. Stalin's contribution to these events was solid but undistinguished. He did his share of dithering at the outset. Once having assented to Lenin's policies, however, he never wavered in his support. He was elected a member of the nine-man Central Committee in April, with the third highest vote (after Lenin and Zinoviev) and remained one of the inner group of leaders throughout the year of revolutionary activity.

Stalin received the relatively junior post of Commissar for Nationalities in the new Soviet Government. His continued importance, however, derived from his being one of a small number of Central Committee members who never deviated from Lenin's policies and who retained his confidence (and his ear) throughout this period. When, therefore, the inner leadership was formalized in 1919 by the creation of a five-man Political Bureau, it was natural that Stalin should gain a place.

The Civil War of 1918-1921 exercised a traumatic effect on the new regime, entrenching methods of rule which contrasted grotesquely with the democratic traditions of the Marxist movement: sharp limitations on freedom of expression and organization, virtual one-party rule, harsh repression of real or suspected opponents of the regime, subordination of the formal organs of government to the party machine, and progressive reduction of the party membership to an appendage of the machine. Among many older party members, especially those in close touch with the workers, there was growing dismay and resentment at the bureaucratization of party processes, and this broke out into open, organized criticism at the end of the Civil War. The leadership, aware of the precariousness of their regime and alarmed at the danger of a party split, reacted by condemning all intra-party opposition as "factionalism," punishable by expulsion. The conversion of the Soviet Republic into a dictatorship of the Politburo was now complete. The key instrument through which this dictatorship was exercised was the highly centralized party machine. In 1921 Stalin, through his position in the Organizational Bureau of the Central

---

[6] Cf. Robert H. McNeal, ed., *The Russian Revolution: Why Did the Bolsheviks Win?* (New York: Holt, Rinehart & Winston, Inc., 1963), and Arthur A. Adams, ed., *The Russian Revolution and Bolshevik Victory: Why and How?* (Boston: D. C. Heath & Company, 1960).

Committee, assumed direction of this machine. In 1922 he was designated Secretary-General of the party.

In the same year, 1922, Lenin suffered the first of a series of strokes, and was capable of only intermittent participation in affairs until his death in January 1924. A struggle for preeminence now set in among his lieutenants.

Why and how did Stalin emerge victorious from this struggle? We have already noted one tremendous advantage he enjoyed: control over the party machine. But surely his colleagues could see the danger of his abusing this power no less than Lenin could, so why did they not take up the suggestion of replacing him? (See below, chap. 4, "Lenin: 'Let's Get Rid of Him' ".) The answer seems to be twofold. On the one hand, effective direction of the machine was crucial to the maintenance of their collective rule, and there was no one else ready and competent to take over this responsibility. On the other hand, Lenin's preeminence had rested not on organizational power but on his personal authority in the party, on his tactical brilliance and the power of his oratory, and the collective rulers were more afraid of an attempt to assert this kind of *personal* authority than they were of Stalin's machine. This miscalculation gave Stalin his chance, and he exploited it superbly. He carefully played on the mutual rivalries and suspicions of his colleagues, placing his organizational power now at the disposal of one group and now of another, acting the man of moderation, modestly implementing the will of the majority—and always keeping open the possibility of changing sides. And while helping his principal rivals to destroy each other, he was assiduously employing his personnel powers first to stack the party congresses with his supporters, then to use the congresses to win a majority on the Central Committee, and finally to use the Central Committee to overrule and then to purge the Politburo. By 1930 the collective dictatorship of the Politburo had been replaced by the personal dictatorship of Josif Stalin.

While the leadership struggles of the 1920s had been articulated in terms of theory and revolutionary strategy, the crucial factors, as we have seen, were organizational power and skill at political in-fighting. The victor could now dictate his own solutions to the theoretical and strategic issues. Could a socialist society be created in "backward" Russia? If so, how? Characteristically, Stalin's solutions were political and organizational. The peasants were forced into state-controlled "collective farms" and obliged to deliver most of their produce to the state at low-fixed prices, industry was entirely nationalized and placed under centralized direction, and prices and wages were fixed so as to maximize capital accumulation at the expense of current consumption. Resistance and criticism were met with mass deportations, executions, and show-trials of "saboteurs." All fields of social activity—economic, educational, artistic, recreational—were placed under centralized organizations whose leaders were directly responsible to Stalin.

Those who supported or served Stalin in the struggles of the 1920s did so from a variety of motives, some idealistic, some less worthy. Few, however, wanted a personal dictatorship. In the upper echelons of the party, misgivings, muted by fear of Stalin's political police, came to a head in 1934, when a clandestine move was set in train to replace him (as Secretary-General) with Sergei Kirov, a Central Committee Secretary and party leader in Leningrad. Stalin was equal to this challenge. On December 1, 1934, Kirov was assassinated, with the connivance of Stalin's secret police. The killing, however, was blamed on a conspiracy of former oppositionists, and the hunt for plotters began. Fear and suspicion, fanned by a massive propaganda machine, reached a crescendo in 1937-38, when most of the Central Committee was arrested. The party apparatus, the officer corps, the government and economic administration, the trade unions, the Communist Youth League, the mass media, the writers' and artists' unions, and finally the political police themselves, all were purged from top to bottom. Scores of thousands were shot and millions were incarcerated in forced labor camps. Meanwhile official propaganda and ideology cast off all semblance of a rational appeal to class interest and Marxist theory, and were transformed to focus on the cult of Stalin. The Soviet regime was now staffed overwhelmingly by young men formed by the Stalin machine and accepting Stalin's absolute personal authority. Stalin's dictatorship had assumed the form it was to retain till his death in 1953. Its three pillars were: (a) total control over all aspects of social life through a system of interlocking bureaucratic hierarchies, directed by members of the dictator's entourage, who were responsible to him alone; (b) prophylactic terror exercised by a secret police network endowed with arbitrary powers of arrest and punishment; and (c) a dogmatized and mythologized ideology, centering around the cult of the leader.

The simultaneous emergence in Germany and Russia of remarkably similar systems of totalitarian dictatorship, despite the greatest contrasts of historical background, social and economic structure, and ideology, presents a problem for which contemporary social science has no agreed solution. Both Hitler and Stalin identified themselves with the interests of the national state, although their immediate programs for furthering these interests differed: Hitler's was foreign aggression, Stalin's economic development. If Hitler was a National Socialist, Stalin was the first National Communist. Original Marxism was strictly internationalist: the proletarian had no fatherland, for his loyalties and antipathies were entirely based on class. Lenin saw his revolution as merely the opening phase of a proletarian revolution that would quickly sweep Europe. To many communists in the 1920s, it seemed axiomatic that the Soviet State existed solely to further the World Revolution. As Stalin's agents extended his authority over the communist parties abroad, however, this relationship was reversed: the way to further the World Revolution was always to place the interests of the Soviet State first. In practise this often meant the sacrifice of revolutionary opportunities or the strengthening of reaction in foreign countries. The ideal Stalinist communist party was a "fifth column" for the U.S.S.R.

The Nazi-Soviet Pact of 1939-41 was the logical expression of Stalin's political style and outlook. As a Leninist, he made no distinction in principle between Nazism and the "bourgeois democracy" of the West: both existed to serve the capitalists. The pact transposed to the international plane the basic tactic used by Stalin in his intra-party struggles, namely, setting his enemies to destroy each other. That this involved a sacrifice of communist parties abroad was a small price for strengthening the Soviet State. This time, however, Stalin's tactic misfired. In 1941 Stalin was not prepared for Hitler's attack and was thrown into confusion and despair when it happened. True, he quickly recovered his balance and pursued with skill and courage the policies of victory. This victory Stalin was later to attribute to the virtues of the Soviet system and to the political and economic policies he pursued in the 1930s. The historian's balance-sheet, however, would note that this system and these policies had both positive and negative effects on Soviet strength and morale, and would give due weight to other factors contributing to victory, such as the patriotism and fortitude of the Russian people, the efforts of Russia's allies, and the political and military miscalculations of the Nazis.

Victory in World War II extended Stalin's power over large areas of Eastern Europe. His objectives here were to establish Soviet patterns of totalitarian control and to maximize direction

from Moscow. As was shown in different ways by his policies toward China and Yugoslavia, he was not interested in communist
regimes he could not himself control. His policies toward the non-
communist world were ones of cautious militancy. The world as
he saw it was now divided into two implacably hostile "camps."
The "imperialist camp" was to be weakened by all means possible
including local and revolutionary wars, while the "socialist camp"
must bend all its efforts toward strengthening its economic and
military might against the ultimate showdown, but that showdown
must be avoided pending the achievement of a preponderance of
power. Internally, Stalin's postwar policies were aimed at keeping
intact the totalitarian dictatorship as it was established in the 1930s.
In 1951-52 he began to prepare a new terroristic purge of the
party and its leadership.

On the eve of Stalin's death, the bankruptcy of his system and
policies were abundantly apparent. His apocalyptic vision of a
two-camp world now a reality, the danger of mutual destruction
was multiplied. Totalitarian controls, terror, and a mythologized
ideology had proved *one* way of initiating industrialization and
modernization, but now they manifestly obstructed further progress
at every turn. New ways forward must be found. These would call
for political skills not inferior to Stalin's—skills, however, deployed
along lines completely foreign to the ex-seminarist turned professional revolutionary, the machine-boss, intriguer, and dictator
Stalin.

Chronology of
the Life of STALIN

1879   (December 21). Born in Gori, Georgia, son of the shoemaker
Vissarion Djugashvili.

1888-93   Studies at Gori Ecclesiastical School.

1890   Father dies.

1894   Enters Tiflis Theological Seminary.

1898   Joins clandestine Social-Democratic group *Messame Dassy*.
Foundation Congress of Russian Social-Democratic Workers'
Party in Minsk.

1899   Expelled from Seminary.

1900   After working briefly in Tiflis Observatory, in danger
of arrest, enters socialist "underground."

1901   Becomes member of Tiflis Social-Democratic Committee.
Transferred to party underground in Batum. An *"Iskra*-man."

1903   Second Congress of Russian Social-Democratic Party: split
into Bolsheviks and Mensheviks.

1902-1904 Arrest, imprisonment in Georgia, exile in Siberia, escape.
Identifies himself as Bolshevik.

1903   Elected *in absentia* to Executive of Transcaucasian
Social-Democratic Federation.

**1904? (or
earlier?)** Marries Ekaterina Svanidze.

1905   Outbreak of Revolution (January). First election to a national
party conference, in Tammerfors.

1905-08   Active in organization of "combat squads" and
"expropriations."

1906   Attends Fourth Congress of Russian Social-Democratic Party·
in Stockholm: first journey abroad.

1907   Death of first wife, leaving son, Vasili.
"Counter-revolution" begins: dispersal of Duma and arrest of
socialist deputies. Stalin attends Fifth Congress of Russian
Social-Democratic Party in London.

1907-08	Active as member of Baku Committee.
1908-09	Arrest, imprisonment in Baku, exile in northern Russia, escape, further activity in Baku.
1910-1913	Repeated imprisonment and exile, with spells of party activity on national level in Petersburg and abroad.
1912	Prague conference of Bolshevik faction—final break with Mensheviks. Stalin co-opted to Central Committee. Made member of four-man Russian Bureau. Editing new Bolshevik newspaper, *Pravda*.
1912-13	Writes "Marxism and the National Question."
1913-17	Exile in northern Siberia.
1917	(March). Downfall of Tsarism. "Dual power" of Provisional Government and Soviets. After brief hesitation, Stalin follows Lenin's policy of "all power to the soviets." Member of Central Committee. (November). Bolsheviks seize power and proclaim a Soviet Republic. Stalin Commissar for Nationalities.
1918-21	Civil War.
1919	Stalin elected member of Political Bureau. Appointed Commissar of Workers' and Peasants' Inspection. Marries Nadezhda Allilueva, daughter of working-class "Old Bolshevik."
1921	Tenth Party Congress: ban on factions. Introduction of New Economic Policy—qualified restoration of private enterprise to restore economy.
1922	Stalin elected Secretary-General of Party.
1924	(January). Death of Lenin. Publication of Stalin's "Foundations of Leninism."
1923-25	In "triumvirate" with Zinoviev and Kamenev, against Trotsky.
1925	Shifts to "Right," forcing Kamenev and Zinoviev into opposition.
1927	Trotsky and Zinoviev expelled from party.
1928	Stalin begins to move against "Right."
1929-30	Replacement of non-Stalinists by Stalinists in all key positions. Stalin now dictator.
1929-33	Forced collectivization of agriculture. First five-year-plan.
1932	Sudden death of wife, believed suicide. Leaves daughter, Svetlana.
1934	Moves in Central Committee to replace Stalin by Kirov. Murder of Kirov. Arrests of "opposition" begin.

applies, inter alia, *to social reforms and improvements, democracy and national liberation.*

3. *The doctrine of the party: the spontaneous aspirations of the workers must be subordinated to the will of a highly disciplined and centralized party, if the Revolution is to be achieved and socialism built.*

These elements of Lenin's thinking form the core of Stalin's political creed. The word creed is used deliberately. Lenin himself appears never to have felt impelled to reduce his basic orientations and ideas to their essentials, or to present them as a simple rounded statement of belief, imbued with an aura of absolute and immutable truth. This was left to the Georgian ex-seminarist. Leninism was the invention of Stalin.

Stalin's article "The Foundations of Leninism," originally published in 1924, contains the most systematic statement of this creed. It is from this article that the following passages are taken.[1]

THE ERA OF IMPERIALISM
AND THE PROLETARIAN REVOLUTION [2]

Leninism is Marxism of the era of imperialism and of the proletarian revolution. To be more exact, Leninism is the theory and tactics of the proletarian revolution in general, the theory and tactics of the dictatorship of the proletariat in particular. Marx and Engels pursued their activities in the pre-revolutionary period (we have the proletarian revolution in mind), when developed imperialism did not yet exist, in the period of the proletarians' preparation for revolution, in the period when the proletarian revolution was not yet an immediate practical inevitability. Lenin, however, the disciple of Marx and Engels, pursued his activities in the period of developed imperialism, in the period of the unfolding proletarian revolution, when the proletarian revolution had already triumphed in one country, had smashed bourgeois democracy and had ushered in the era of proletarian democracy, the era of the Soviets. . . .

Between Marx and Engels, on the one hand, and Lenin, on the

[1] "The Foundations of Leninism: Lectures Delivered at the Sverdlov University in the Beginning of April, 1929," in J. Stalin, *Problems of Leninism* (Moscow, 1945), pp. 14, 20, 21, 29-31, 37-39, 42, 43, 45, 46, 48-50, 57, 61, 62, 69-71, 78, 79, 81-93.

[2] Section headings here and throughout are the editor's.

1937-38	Culmination of purge—the "Yezhovshchina"; Old Bolsheviks killed.
1939-41	Pact with Hitler.
1941-45	Nazi invasion; U.S.S.R. allied with Britain and the United States. After defeat of Germany Stalin enters war against Japan.
1945-48	Establishment of Soviet "satellites" in Eastern Europe.
1948	Tito's Yugoslavia succeeds in asserting independence.
1949	Establishment of Chinese People's Republic.
1950	Communists launch Korean war. Publication of Stalin's "Marxism and Questions of Linguistics."
1951-52	Change of Political Police chief and arrests in Georgia mark first moves in new purge.
1952	Stalin's "Economic Problems of Communism." Nineteenth Party Congress: reorganization of central organs of party.
1953	(January). "Doctors' plot" arrests announced. (March 5). Death of Stalin. (March 9). Embalmed body placed in Lenin Mausoleum.
1956	Twentieth Party Congress: Khrushchev's "secret speech" and condemnation of "cult of personality."
1961	Twenty-Second Party Congress: further criticism of Stalin; body removed from Mausoleum.

STALIN LOOKS AT THE WORLD

1

The Foundations of Stalinism

Stalin was a man of action rather than a creative thinker. Russian Marxism, however, demanded of its leaders not only that they master "theory," but also that they justify their policies and strategies and fight out their differences in terms of "theory." It is to this tradition that we owe Stalin's theoretical writings, which constitute at the same time a claim to leadership and the rationalization of a political career. On points of detail, Stalin showed a striking readiness to adapt his theoretical position to the demands of expediency. There is, however, a stable groundwork of ideas, ideas derived originally from Marx and Lenin but re-ordered in his own mind, which can be identified as Stalin's political creed.

Stalin's critics have commented adversely on the pedestrian quality of his thought and expression. Others, however, have noted his ability to reduce a complex body of facts or ideas to a coherent system presented clearly and unambiguously. Is this a genius for getting at the essence of things, or a genius for vulgarization, as has sometimes been alleged?

What cannot be doubted is Stalin's grasp of what was new and specific in Lenin's Marxism. This we may summarize as follows:

1. Emphasis on revolutionary will and political activism, against those Marxists who stressed the dependence of political change on the "maturing" of social and economic conditions.
2. Extreme relativism in appraising social forces and values: these are good only when and insofar as they serve the Revolution. This

other, there lies a whole period of domination of the opportunism of the Second International. . . . This was the period of the relatively peaceful development of capitalism, the pre-war period, so to speak, when the catastrophic contradictions of imperialism had not yet become so glaringly evident, when workers' economic strikes and trade unions were developing more or less "normally," when election campaigns and parliamentary parties yielded "dizzying" successes, when legal forms of struggle were lauded to the skies, and when it was thought that capitalism would be "killed" by legal means—in short, when the parties of the Second International were vegetating and there was no inclination to think seriously about revolution, about the dictatorship of the proletariat, or about the revolutionary education of the masses. . . .

Meanwhile, a new period of imperialist wars and of revolutionary battles of the proletariat was approaching. The old methods of fighting were proving obviously inadequate and impotent in face of the omnipotence of finance capital. . . . The honour of bringing about this general overhauling and general cleansing of the Augean stables of the Second International fell to Leninism. . . .

The theory of the proletarian revolution. The Leninist theory of the proletarian revolution proceeds from three fundamental theses.

First Thesis: The domination of finance capital in the advanced capitalist countries; the issue of stocks and bonds as one of the principal operations of finance capital; the export of capital to the sources of raw materials, which is one of the foundations of imperialism; the omnipotence of a financial oligarchy, which is the result of the domination of finance capital—all this reveals the grossly parasitic character of monopolist capitalism, makes the yoke of the capitalist trusts and syndicates a hundred times more burdensome, quickens the revolt of the working class against the foundations of capitalism, and brings the masses to the proletarian revolution as their only salvation. (*Cf.* Lenin, *Imperialism, the Highest Stage of Capitalism.*)

Hence the first conclusion: intensification of the revolutionary crisis within the capitalist countries and growth of the elements of an explosion on the internal, proletarian front in the "mother countries."

Second Thesis: The increase in the export of capital to the colonies and dependent countries; the extension of "spheres of influence" and colonial possessions until they cover the whole globe; the transformation of capitalism into a *world system* of financial enslavement and colonial oppression of the vast majority of the population of the earth by a handful of "advanced" countries—all this has, on the one hand, converted the separate national economies and national territories into links in a single chain called world economy and, on the other hand, split the population of the globe into two camps: a handful of "advanced" capitalist countries which exploit and oppress vast colonies and dependencies, and the vast majority of colonial and dependent countries which are compelled to fight for their liberation from the imperialist yoke. (*Cf.* Lenin, *Imperialism*.) . . .

Hence the second conclusion: intensification of the revolutionary crisis in the colonial countries and growth of the elements of revolt against imperialism on the external, colonial front.

Third Thesis: The monopolistic possession of "spheres of influence" and colonies; the uneven development of the different capitalist countries, leading to a frenzied struggle for the redivision of the world between the countries which have already seized territories and those claiming their "share"; imperialist wars as the only method of restoring the disturbed "equilibrium"—all this leads to the aggravation of the third front, the inter-capitalist front, which weakens imperialsm and facilitates the amalgamation of the first two fronts against imperialism: the front of the revolutionary proletariat and the front of colonial emancipation. (*Cf. Imperialism*.)

Hence the third conclusion: that under imperialism wars cannot be averted, and that a coalition between the proletarian revolution in Europe and the colonial revolution in the East in a united world front of revolution against the world front of imperialism is inevitable. . . .

Where will the revolution begin? Where, in what country, can the front of capital be pierced first?

Where industry is more developed, where the proletariat constitutes the majority, where there is more culture, where there is more democracy—that was the reply usually given formerly.

No, objects the Leninist theory of revolution; *not necessarily where industry is more developed*, and so forth. The front of capital will be pierced where the chain of imperialism is weakest, for the proletarian revolution is the result of the breaking of the chain of the world imperialist front at its weakest link; and it may turn out that the country which has started the revolution, which has made a breach in the front of capital, is less developed in a capitalist sense than other, more developed, countries, which have, however, remained within the framework of capitalism.

In 1917 the chain of the imperialist world front proved to be weaker in Russia than in the other countries. It was there that the chain gave way and provided an outlet for the proletarian revolution. . . .

To proceed. Formerly, the victory of the revolution in one country was considered impossible, on the assumption that it would require the combined action of the proletarians of all or at least of a majority of the advanced countries to achieve victory over the bourgeoisie. Now this point of view no longer accords with the facts. Now we must proceed from the possibility of such a victory, for the uneven and spasmodic character of the development of the various capitalist countries under the conditions of imperialism, the development, within imperialism, of catastrophic contradictions leading to inevitable wars, the growth of the revolutionary movement in all countries of the world—all this leads, not only to the possibility, but also to the necessity of the victory of the proletariat in individual countries. The history of the Russian Revolution is direct proof of this. . . .

But the overthrow of the power of the bourgeoisie and establishment of the power of the proletariat in one country does not yet mean that the complete victory of Socialism has been ensured. After consolidating its power and taking the peasantry in tow, the proletariat of the victorious country can and must build up a Socialist society. But does this mean that it will thereby achieve the complete and final victory of Socialism, *i.e.*, does it mean that with the forces of only one country it can finally consolidate Socialism and fully guarantee that country against intervention and, consequently, also against restoration? No, it does not. For this the victory of the revolution in at least several countries is needed. Therefore, the development and support of revolution in other countries is an essential task of the victorious revolution. Therefore, the revolution in the victorious country must regard itself not as a self-sufficient entity but as an aid, as a means of hastening the victory of the proletariat in other countries. . . .

THE DICTATORSHIP
OF THE PROLETARIAT

1. *The dictatorship of the proletariat as the instrument of the proletarian revolution.* The question of the proletarian dictatorship is above all a question of the main content of the proletarian revo-

lution. The proletarian revolution, its movement, its scope and its achievements acquire flesh and blood only through the dictatorship of the proletariat. The dictatorship of the proletariat is the instrument of the proletarian revolution, its organ, its most important mainstay, brought into being for the purpose of, firstly, crushing the resistance of the overthrown exploiters and consolidating the achievements of the proletarian revolution, and, secondly, carrying the proletarian revolution to its completion, carrying the revolution to the complete victory of Socialism. The revolution can vanquish the bourgeoisie, can overthrow its power, without the dictatorship of the proletariat. But the revolution will be unable to crush the resistance of the bourgeoisie, to maintain its victory and to push forward to the final victory of Socialism unless, at a certain stage in its development, it creates a special organ in the form of the dictatorship of the proletariat as its principal mainstay. . . .

2. *The dictatorship of the proletariat as the domination of the proletariat over the bourgeoisie.* . . . The dictatorship of the proletariat arises not on the basis of the bourgeois order, but in the process of the breaking up of this order after the overthrow of the bourgeoisie, in the process of the expropriation of the landlords and capitalists, in the process of the socialization of the principal instruments and means of production, in the process of violent proletarian revolution. The dictatorship of the proletariat is a revolutionary power based on the use of force against the bourgeoisie. . . .

In other words, the law of violent proletarian revolution, the law of the smashing of the bourgeois state machine as a preliminary condition for such a revolution, is an inevitable law of the revolutionary movement in the imperialist countries of the world.

Of course, in the remote future, if the proletariat is victorious in the most important capitalist countries, and if the present capitalist encirclement is replaced by a Socialist encirclement, a "peaceful" path of development is quite possible for certain capitalist countries, whose capitalists, in view of the "unfavourable" international situation, will consider it expedient "voluntarily" to make substantial concessions to the proletariat. But this supposition applies only to a remote and possible future. . . .

3. *The Soviet power as the state form of the dictatorship of the proletariat.* The victory of the dictatorship of the proletariat signifies the suppression of the bourgeoisie, the smashing of the bourgeois state machine, and the substitution of proletarian democracy

for bourgeois democracy. That is clear. But by means of what organizations can this colossal task be carried out? . . . This new form of organization of the proletariat is the Soviets. . . .

THE PEASANT
AND NATIONAL PROBLEMS

Some think that the fundamental thing in Leninism is the peasant problem, that the point of departure of Leninism is the problem of the peasantry, of its role and relative importance. This is absolutely wrong. The fundamental problem of Leninism, its point of departure, is not the peasant problem, but the problem of the dictatorship of the proletariat, of the conditions under which it can be achieved, of the conditions under which it can be consolidated. The peasant problem, as the problem of the ally of the proletariat in its struggle for power, is a derivative problem. . . .

The question presents itself as follows: Are the revolutionary possibilities latent in the peasantry by virtue of certain conditions of its existence *already exhausted,* or not; and if not, *is there any hope, any basis,* for utilizing these possibilities *for* the proletarian revolution, for transforming the peasantry, the exploited majority of it, from the reserve of the bourgeoisie which it was during the bourgeois revolutions in the West and still is even now, into a reserve of the proletariat, into its ally?

Leninism replies to this question in the affirmative, *i.e.,* to the effect that it recognizes the existence of revolutionary capabilities in the ranks of the majority of the peasantry, and to the effect that it is possible to use these in the interests of the proletarian dictatorship. The history of the three revolutions in Russia fully corroborates the conclusions of Leninism on this score. . . .

Lenin rightly pointed out in his articles on cooperation that the development of agriculture in our country must proceed along a new path, along the path of drawing the majority of the peasants into Socialist construction through the cooperative societies, along the path of gradually introducing into agriculture the principles of collectivism, first in the sphere of marketing and later in the sphere of production of agricultural products. . . .

Formerly, the national problem was regarded from a reformist point of view, as an independent problem having no connection with the general problems of the rule of capital, of the overthrow of imperialism, of the proletarian revolution. It was tacitly assumed that the victory of the proletariat in Europe was possible without a direct alliance with the liberation movement in the colonies, that the national-colonial problem could be solved on the quiet, "of its own accord," off the high road of the proletarian revolution, without a revolutionary struggle against imperialism. Now we can say that this anti-revolutionary point of view has been exposed. Leninism has proved, and the imperialist war and the revolution in Russia have confirmed, that the national problem can be solved only in connection with and on the basis of the proletarian revolution, and that the road to victory of the revolution in the West lies through the revolutionary alliance with the liberation movement of the colonies and dependent countries against imperialism. The national problem is a part of the general problem of the proletarian revolution, a part of the problem of the dictatorship of the proletariat.

The question presents itself as follows: Are the revolutionary possibilities latent in the revolutionary liberation movement of the oppressed countries *already exhausted* or not; and if not, is there any hope, any ground to expect that these possibilities can be utilized for the proletarian revolution, that the dependent and colonial countries can be transformed from a reserve of the imperialist bourgeoisie into a reserve of the revolutionary proletariat, into an ally of the latter?

Leninism replies to this question in the affirmative, *i.e.*, to the effect that it recognizes the latent revolutionary capabilities of the national liberation movement of the oppressed countries, and to the effect that it is possible to use these for the purpose of overthrowing the common enemy, for the purpose of overthrowing imperialism. The mechanics of the development of imperialism, the imperialist war and the revolution in Russia wholly confirm the conclusions of Leninism on this score.

Hence the necessity for the proletariat to support—resolutely and actively to support—the national liberation movement of the oppressed and dependent peoples.

This does not mean, of course, that the proletariat must support *every* national movement, everywhere and always, in every single concrete case. It means that support must be given to such national movements as tend to weaken, to overthrow imperialism, and not to strengthen and preserve it. Cases occur when the national movements in certain oppressed countries come into conflict with the interests of the development of the proletarian movement.

In such cases support is, of course, entirely out of the question. The question of the rights of nations is not an isolated, self-sufficient question; it is a part of the general problem of the proletarian revolution, subordinate to the whole, and must be considered from the point of view of the whole. . . .

STRATEGY AND TACTICS

Our revolution already passed through two stages, and after the October Revolution it has entered a third stage. Our strategy changed accordingly. . . .

Third stage. Commenced after the October Revolution. Objective: to consolidate the dictatorship of the proletariat in one country, using it as a base for the overthrow of imperialism in all countries. The revolution is spreading beyond the confines of one country; the epoch of world revolution has commenced. The main forces of the revolution: the dictatorship of the proletariat in one country, the revolutionary movement of the proletariat in all countries. Main reserves: the semi-proletarian and small-peasant masses in the developed countries, the liberation movement in the colonies and dependent countries. Direction of the main blow: isolation of the petty-bourgeois democrats, isolation of the parties of the Second International, which constitute the main support of the policy of *compromise* with imperialism. Plan for the disposition of forces: alliance of the proletarian revolution with the liberation movement in the colonies and the dependent countries.

Strategy deals with the main forces of the revolution and their reserves. It changes with the passing of the revolution from one stage to another, but remains essentially unchanged throughout a given stage. . . .

Tactics deal with the forms of struggle and the forms of organization of the proletariat, with their changes and combinations. During a given stage of the revolution tactics may change several times, depending on the flow or ebb, the rise or decline, of the revolution.

Strategic leadership. The reserves of the revolution can be:

Direct: a) the peasantry and in general the intermediate strata of the population within the country; b) the proletariat of the neighbouring countries; c) the revolutionary movement in the colonies and dependent countries; d) the gains and achievements of the dictatorship of the proletariat—part of which the proletariat may give up temporarily, while retaining superiority of forces, in order to buy off a powerful enemy and gain a respite; and

Indirect: a) the contradictions and conflicts among the non-proletarian classes within the country, which can be utilized by the proletariat to weaken the enemy and to strengthen its own reserves; b) contradictions, conflicts and wars (the imperialist war, for instance) among the bourgeois states hostile to the proletarian state, which can be utilized by the proletariat in its offensive or in manœuvring in the event of a forced retreat. . . .

Reformism and revolutionism. What is the difference between revolutionary tactics and reformist tactics? . . .

To a reformist, reforms are everything, while revolutionary work is something incidental, something just to talk about, mere eyewash. That is why, with reformist tactics under the bourgeois regime, reforms are inevitably transformed into an instrument for strengthening that regime, an instrument for disintegrating the revolution. . . .

To a revolutionary, on the contrary, the main thing is revolutionary work and not reforms; to him reforms are by-products of the revolution. That is why, with revolutionary tactics under the bourgeois regime, reforms are naturally transformed into instruments for disintegrating this regime, into instruments for strengthening the revolution, into a base for the further development of the revolutionary movement.

The revolutionary will accept a reform in order to use it as an aid in combining legal work with illegal work, to intensify, under its cover, the illegal work for the revolutionary preparation of the masses for the overthrow of the bourgeoisie.

This is what making revolutionary use of reforms and agreements under the conditions of imperialism means. . . .

THE PARTY

What are the specific features of this new party?

1. *The Party as the vanguard of the working class.* The Party must be, first of all, the *vanguard* of the working class. The Party must absorb all the best elements of the working class, their experience, their revolutionary spirit, their selfless devotion to the cause of the proletariat. But in order that it may really be the vanguard, the Party must be armed with revolutionary theory, with a knowledge of the laws of the movement, with a knowledge

of the laws of revolution. Without this it will be incapable of directing the struggle of the proletariat, of leading the proletariat. The Party cannot be a real party if it limits itself to registering what the masses of the working class feel and think, if it drags at the tail of the spontaneous movement, if it is unable to overcome the inertness and the political indifference of the spontaneous movement, if it is unable to rise above the momentary interests of the proletariat, if it is unable to elevate the masses to the level of the class interests of the proletariat. The Party must stand at the head of the working class; it must see farther than the working class; it must lead the proletariat, and not follow in the tail of the spontaneous movement. . . .

No army at war can dispense with an experienced General Staff if it does not want to court certain defeat. Is it not clear that the proletariat can still less dispense with such a General Staff if it does not want to give itself up to be devoured by its mortal enemies? But where is this General Staff? Only the revolutionary party of the proletariat can serve as this General Staff. The working class without a revolutionary party is an army without a General Staff. The Party is the General Staff of the proletariat. . . .

2. *The Party as the organized detachment of the working class.* The Party is not only the *vanguard* detachment of the working class. If it desires really to direct the struggle of the class it must at the same time be the *organized* detachment of its class. The Party's tasks under the conditions of capitalism are extremely serious and varied. . . . But the Party can fulfill these tasks only if it is itself the embodiment of discipline and organization. . . .

The principle of the minority submitting to the majority, the principle of directing Party work from a centre, not infrequently gives rise to attacks on the part of wavering elements, to accusations of "bureaucracy," "formalism," etc. It need hardly be proved that systematic work by the Party, as one whole, and the directing of the struggle of the working class would have been impossible if these principles had not been adhered to. Leninism in the organizational question means unswerving application of these principles. . . .

3. *The Party as the highest form of class organization of the proletariat.* The Party is the organized detachment of the working class. But the Party is not the only organization of the working class. The proletariat has also a number of other organizations, without which it cannot properly wage the struggle against capital: trade unions, cooperative societies, factory and works organiza-

tions, parliamentary groups, non-Party women's associations, the press, cultural and educational organizations, youth leagues, revolutionary fighting organizations (in times of open revolutionary action), Soviets of deputies as the form of state organization (if the proletariat is in power), etc. The overwhelming majority of these organizations are non-Party, and only a certain part of them adhere directly to the Party, or represent its offshoots. . . .

The question then arises: who is to determine the line, the general direction, along which the work of all these organizations is to be conducted? . . .

This organization is the Party of the proletariat . . . the Party, as the best school for training leaders of the working class, is, by reason of its experience and prestige, the only organization capable of centralizing the leadership of the struggle of the proletariat, thus transforming each and every non-Party organization of the working class into an auxiliary body and transmission belt linking the Party with the class. The Party is the highest form of class organization of the proletariat. . . .

4. *The Party as the instrument of the dictatorship of the proletariat.* . . . The Party is not only the highest form of class association of the proletarians; it is at the same time an *instrument* in the hands of the proletariat *for* achieving the dictatorship where that has not yet been achieved and *for* consolidating and expanding the dictatorship where it has already been achieved. . . .

The proletariat needs the Party *for* the purpose of achieving and maintaining the dictatorship. The Party is an instrument of the dictatorship of the proletariat.

But from this it follows that when classes disappear and the dictatorship of the proletariat withers away, the Party will also wither away.

5. *The Party as the embodiment of unity of will, incompatible with the existence of factions.* The achievement and maintenance of the dictatorship of the proletariat is impossible without a party which is strong by reason of its solidarity and iron discipline. . . . Iron discipline does not preclude but presupposes conscious and voluntary submission, for only conscious discipline can be truly iron discipline. But after a contest of opinion has been closed, after criticism has been exhausted and a decision has been arrived at, unity of will and unity of action of all Party members are the necessary conditions without which neither Party unity nor iron discipline in the Party is conceivable. . . .

But from this it follows that the existence of factions is incompatible either with the Party's unity or with its iron discipline. It need hardly be proved that the existence of factions leads to the existence of a number of centres, and the existence of a number of centres connotes the absence of one common centre in the Party, the breaking up of the unity of will, the weakening and disintegration of discipline, the weakening and disintegration of the dictatorship. Of course, the parties of the Second International, which are fighting against the dictatorship of the proletariat and have no desire to lead the proletarians to power, can afford such liberalism as freedom of factions, for they have no need at all for iron discipline. But the parties of the Communist International, which base their activities on the task of achieving and consolidating the dictatorship of the proletariat, cannot afford to be "liberal" or to permit freedom of factions. The Party represents unity of will, which precludes all factionalism and division of authority in the Party. . . .

6. *The Party is strengthened by purging itself of opportunist elements.* The source of factionalism in the Party is its opportunist elements. . . . Our Party succeeded in creating internal unity and unexampled cohesion of its ranks primarily because it was able in good time to purge itself of the opportunist pollution, because it was able to rid its ranks of the Liquidators, the Mensheviks. Proletarian parties develop and become strong by purging themselves of opportunists and reformists, social-imperialists and social-chauvinists, social-patriots, and social-pacifists. The Party becomes strong by purging itself of opportunist elements. . . .

STYLE IN WORK

Leninism is a school of theory and practice which trains a special type of Party and state worker, creates a special Leninist style in work. What are the characteristic features of this style? What are its peculiarities?

It has two specific features: a) the Russian revolutionary sweep and b) American efficiency. The style of Leninism is a combination of these two specific features in Party and state work.

The Russian revolutionary sweep is an antidote to inertness, routine, conservatism, mental stagnation and slavish submission to ancestral traditions. The Russian revolutionary sweep is the life-giving force which stimulates thought, impels things forward, breaks the past and opens up perspectives. Without it no progress is possible. But there is every chance of it degenerating in practice into empty "revolutionary" Manilovism[3] if it is not combined with American efficiency in work. . . . American efficiency is that indomitable force which neither knows nor recognizes obstacles; which with its business-like perseverance brushes aside all obstacles; which continues at a task once started until it is finished, even if it is a minor task; and without which serious constructive work is inconceivable. But American efficiency has every chance of degenerating into narrow and unprincipled commercialism if it is not combined with the Russian revolutionary sweep.

[3] The allusion is to a character in Gogol's novel *Dead Souls*. Manilovism, implying abstract theorizing and impracticality, was a term of disdain in the Russian revolutionary movement.

2
Stalin Speaks

In this chapter we present examples of Stalin's public style in almost the full range of communication situations: the party congress speech, funeral oration, party polemic, theoretical article, election speech, personal interview, and radio talk. A number of the extracts supplement the exposition of Stalin's creed in the previous chapter by presenting his views on major topics on which he figured as innovator: the state under communism, Soviet patriotism, the intelligentsia, and "basis and superstructure."

WHY I BECAME
A REVOLUTIONARY

There is extremely little autobiographical information in Stalin's recorded statements and writings. The present passage and the next constitute the most interesting known references to his early years and career in the revolutionary underground. While they can be taken as direct evidence only of how he wished to present his past, they also constitute practically our only evidence, difficult to assess though it be, of how he actually viewed it.[1]

Ludwig: Allow me to put a few questions to you concerning your biography. When I went to see Masaryk he told me he was conscious of being a Socialist when only six years old. What made you a Socialist and when was that?

[1] Extract from an interview given to the German biographer and journalist Emil Ludwig, on December 13, 1931. See J. V. Stalin, *Works*, XIII (Moscow, 1955), 115-16.

Stalin: I cannot assert that I was already drawn to socialism at the age of six. Not even at the age of ten or twelve. I joined the revolutionary movement when fifteen years old, when I became connected with underground groups of Russian Marxists then living in Transcaucasia. These groups exerted great influence on me and instilled in me a taste for underground Marxist literature.

Ludwig: What impelled you to become an oppositionist? Was it, perhaps, bad treatment by your parents?

Stalin: No. My parents were uneducated, but they did not treat me badly by any means. But it was a different matter at the Orthodox theological seminary which I was then attending. In protest against the outrageous regime and the jesuitical methods prevalent at the seminary, I was ready to become, and actually did become, a revolutionary, a believer in Marxism as a really revolutionary teaching.

Ludwig: But do you not admit that the Jesuits have good points?

Stalin: Yes, they are systematic and persevering in working to achieve sordid ends. But their principal method is spying, prying, worming their way into people's souls and outraging their feelings. What good can there be in that? For instance, the spying in the hostel. At nine o'clock the bell rings for morning tea, we go to the dining-room, and when we return to our rooms we find that meantime a search has been made and all our chests have been ransacked. . . . What good point can there be in that?

MY REVOLUTIONARY APPRENTICESHIP [2]

Let me turn back to the past.

I recall the year 1898, when I was first put in charge of a study circle of workers from the railway workshops. That was some twenty-eight years ago. I recall the days when in the home of Comrade Sturua, and in the presence of Djibladze (he was also one of my teachers at that time), Chodrishvili, Chkheidze, Bochorishvili, Ninua and other advanced workers of Tiflis, I received my first lessons in practical work. Compared with these comrades, I was then quite a young man. I may have been a little better-read than many of them were, but as a practical worker I was unquestionably a novice in those days. It was here, among these comrades, that I

[2] From a speech in reply to greetings given at a meeting of railway workers in Tiflis in 1926. *Ibid.,* VIII (Moscow, 1954), 183-84.

received my first baptism in the revolutionary struggle. It was here, among these comrades, that I became an apprentice in the art of revolution. As you see, my first teachers were Tiflis workers.

Permit me to tender them my sincere comradely thanks. (*Applause.*)

I recall, further, the years 1907-09, when, by the will of the Party, I was transferred to work in Baku. Three years of revolutionary activity among the workers in the oil industry steeled me as a practical fighter and as one of the local practical leaders. Association with such advanced workers in Baku as Vatsek, Saratovets, Fioletov and others, on the one hand, and the storm of acute conflicts between the workers and the oil owners, on the other, first taught me what it means to lead large masses of workers. It was there, in Baku, that I thus received my second baptism in the revolutionary struggle. There I became a journeyman in the art of revolution.

Permit me to tender my sincere comradely thanks to my Baku teachers. (*Applause.*)

Lastly, I recall the year 1917, when, by the will of the Party, after my wanderings from one prison and place of exile to another, I was transferred to Leningrad. There, in the society of Russian workers, and in direct contact with Comrade Lenin, the great teacher of the proletarians of all countries, in the storm of mighty clashes between the proletariat and the bourgeoisie, in the conditions of the imperialist war, I first learnt what it means to be one of the leaders of the great Party of the working class. There, in the society of Russian workers—the liberators of oppressed peoples and the pioneers of the proletarian struggle of all countries and all peoples—I received my third baptism in the revolutionary struggle. There, in Russia, under Lenin's guidance, I became a master workman in the art of revolution.

Permit me to tender my sincere comradely thanks to my Russian teachers and to bow my head in homage to the memory of my great teacher—Lenin. (*Applause.*)

From the rank of apprentice (Tiflis), to the rank of journeyman (Baku), and then to the rank of a master workman of our revolution (Leningrad)—such, comrades, was the school in which I passed my revolutionary apprenticeship.

Such, comrades, is the true picture of what I was and what I have become, if one is to speak without exaggeration and in all conscience. (*Applause rising to a stormy ovation.*)

A LENIN LITANY

Stalin was unique among the leaders of Bolshevism in hav-ing received an exclusively ecclesiastical education, whose imprint on his characteristic modes of thought and expression have frequently been noted. The legacy of the seminary was particularly apparent when Stalin sought to achieve emphasis or to convey solemnity or emotion; here his usual recourse was to hyperbolic biblical imagery or the throbbing repeti-tion of a litany, which presented a striking contrast to the rational, matter-of-fact style traditional in the Marxist move-ment. On January 26, 1924, Stalin startled his audience at a special meeting of the All-Union Congress of Soviets held to mark the funeral of Lenin, by giving an unusually forceful and extended display of his litany style. Treating each area of party policy in turn, he wound up with a series of "vows" addressed to the departed leader, which we reproduce below. Here Stalin sketches the outline of the Lenin cult, which later formed the model and basis of the cult of Stalin himself.[3]

Departing from us, Comrade Lenin enjoined us to hold high and guard the purity of the great title of member of the Party. We vow to you, Comrade Lenin, that we shall fulfil your behest with honour! . . .

Departing from us, Comrade Lenin enjoined us to guard the unity of our Party as the apple of our eye. We vow to you, Com-rade Lenin, that this behest, too, we shall fulfil with honour! . . .

Departing from us, Comrade Lenin enjoined us to guard and strengthen the dictatorship of the proletariat. We vow to you, Comrade Lenin, that we shall spare no effort to fulfil this behest, too, with honour! . . .

Departing from us, Comrade Lenin enjoined us to strengthen with all our might the alliance of the workers and peasants. We vow to you, Comrade Lenin, that this behest, too, we shall fulfil with honour! . . .

Departing from us, Comrade Lenin enjoined us to strengthen and extend the union of republics. We vow to you, Comrade Lenin, that this behest, too, we shall fulfil with honour! . . .

[3] *Ibid.*, VI (Moscow, 1953), 47-53.

Departing from us, Comrade Lenin enjoined us to remain faithful to the principles of the Communist International. We vow to you, Comrade Lenin, that we shall not spare our lives to strengthen and extend the union of the working people of the whole world—the Communist International!

HOW TO DEAL
WITH OPPOSITION

The following passage from Stalin's speech to the Fifteenth Congress in 1927, when he was already well on the way to establishing his dominance, illustrates his style of intra-party polemic and employs some of his favorite operational concepts. There is one true path ahead, and typically one true leader to light the way. The party is a living organism. Those who commit the cardinal sin of opposing the impersonal forces of history must expect to suffer for it. In contrast to Lenin, who retained his personal respect for old comrades with whom he had parted company and was ready to yank back into "the cart" any who momentarily fell from it, Stalin contemplates the spectacle of fallen comrades with scarcely concealed glee. A decade later he was to exterminate them.[4]

From Kamenev's speech it is evident that the opposition does not intend to disarm completely. The opposition's declaration of December 3 indicates the same thing. Evidently, the opposition prefers to be outside the Party. Well, let it be outside the Party. There is nothing terrible, or exceptional, or surprising, in the fact that they prefer to be outside the Party, that they are cutting themselves off from the Party. If you study the history of our Party you will find that always, at certain serious turns taken by our Party, a certain section of the old leaders fell out of the cart of the Bolshevik Party and made room for new people. A turn is a serious thing, comrades. A turn is dangerous for those who do not sit firmly in the Party cart. Not everybody can keep his balance when a turn is made. You turn the cart—and on looking round you find that somebody has fallen out. (*Applause.*)

Let us take 1903, the period of the Second Congress of our Party. That was the period of the Party's turn from agreement with the

[4] *Ibid.*, X (Moscow, 1954), 379-82.

liberals to a mortal struggle against the liberal bourgeoisie, from preparing for the struggle against tsarism to open struggle against it for completely routing tsarism and feudalism. At that time the Party was headed by the six: Plekhanov, Zasulich, Martov, Lenin, Axelrod and Potresov. The turn proved fatal to five out of the six. They fell out of the cart. Lenin alone remained. (*Applause.*) It turned out that the old leaders of the Party, the founders of the Party (Plekhanov, Zasulich and Axelrod) plus two young ones (Martov and Potresov) were against one, also a young one, Lenin. If only you knew how much howling, weeping and wailing there was then that the Party was doomed, that the Party would not hold out, that nothing could be done without the old leaders. The howling and wailing subsided, however, but the facts remained. And the facts were that precisely thanks to the departure of the five the Party succeeded in getting on to the right road. It is now clear to every Bolshevik that if Lenin had not waged a resolute struggle against the five, if the five had not been pushed aside, our Party could not have rallied as a Bolshevik Party capable of leading the proletarians to the revolution against the bourgeoisie. (*Voices:* "That's true!")

Let us take the next period, the period 1907-08. That was the period of our Party's turn from open revolutionary struggle against tsarism to flanking methods of struggle, to the use of all kinds of legal possibilities—from insurance funds to the floor of the Duma. It was the period of retreat after we had been defeated in the 1905 Revolution. This turn required of us that we should master new methods of struggle in order, after mustering our forces, to resume the open revolutionary struggle against tsarism. But this turn proved fatal to a number of old Bolsheviks. Alexinsky fell out of the cart. At one time he was quite a good Bolshevik. Bogdanov fell out. He was one of the most prominent leaders of our Party. Rozhkov—a former member of the Central Committee of our Party—fell out. And so forth. There was, perhaps, at that time no less howling and wailing that the Party would perish than in 1903. The howling, however, subsided but the facts remained. And the facts showed that the Party would not have been able to get on to the right road under the new conditions of struggle had it not purged itself of the people who were wavering and hindering the cause of the revolution. What was Lenin's object at that time? He had only one object: to rid the Party of the unstable and whining elements as quickly as possible, so that they should not get in our way. (*Applause.*)

That is how our Party grew, comrades.

Our Party is a living organism. Like every organism, it undergoes a process of metabolism: the old and obsolete passes away (*applause*), the new and growing lives and develops. (*Applause.*) Some go away, both at the top and at the bottom. New ones grow, both at the top and at the bottom, and lead the cause forward. That is how our Party grew. That is how it will continue to grow.

The same must be said about the present period of our revolution. We are in the period of a turn from the restoration of industry and agriculture to the reconstruction of the entire national economy, to its reconstruction on a new technical basis, when the building of socialism is no longer merely in prospect, but a living, practical matter, which calls for the surmounting of extremely great difficulties of an internal and external character.

You know that this turn has proved fatal to the leaders of our opposition, who were scared by the new difficulties and intended to turn the Party in the direction of surrender. And if certain leaders, who do not want to sit firmly in the cart, now fall out, it is nothing to be surprised at. It will merely rid the Party of people who are getting in its way and hindering its progress. Evidently, they seriously want to free themselves from our Party cart. Well, if some of the old leaders who are turning into trash intend to fall out of the cart—a good riddance to them! (*Stormy and prolonged applause. The whole congress rises and gives Comrade Stalin an ovation.*)

THE FUTURE COMMUNIST SOCIETY

Here Stalin presents his image of the ideal communist society, toward which all the policies of his regime and all the efforts and sufferings of the Soviet people were held to be directed. This "higher" stage of communism was to be preceded by an indefinite period at a lower stage ("socialism"), during which the "material and spiritual prerequisites" of communism were to be created. The passage is taken from an interview given to an American "Labor Delegation" in 1927.[5]

The general characteristics of communist society are given in the works of Marx, Engels and Lenin.

Briefly, the anatomy of communist society may be described as

[5] *Ibid.*, pp. 139-40.

follows: It is a society in which: a) there will be no private ownership of the instruments and means of production, but social, collective ownership; b) there will be no classes or state power, but there will be working people in industry and agriculture who manage economic affairs as a free association of working people; c) the national economy, organized according to plan, will be based on the highest level of technique, both in industry and agriculture; d) there will be no antithesis between town and country, between industry and agriculture; e) products will be distributed according to the principle of the old French Communists: "from each according to his ability, to each according to his needs"; f) science and art will enjoy conditions sufficiently favorable for them to attain full flowering; g) the individual, freed from concern about his daily bread and from the necessity of adapting himself to the "powers that be," will become really free.

THE STATE UNDER COMMUNISM

Marx and Engels regarded the state as an instrument for the systematic use of violence, employed by a ruling class to maintain its dominance and the property relations through which its exploitation of the masses was realized. Hence in the classless society of communism there would be no need for the state, which would wither away. Lenin amended this picture by stressing the importance of the phase known as "the dictatorship of the proletariat" during which the "proletariat" would require a state of its own in order to combat counterrevolution and to create the necessary conditions for communism. In 1937, during the Yezhovshchina, *Stalin justified the intensification of the repressive activities of the Soviet state with the doctrine that the class struggle grows more bitter the nearer the proletariat gets to complete victory. In 1939 at the Eighteenth Party Congress, he went a step further and stated that the state would continue to exist even under full communism, provided there was still a "capitalist encirclement."* [6]

It is sometimes asked: "We have abolished the exploiting classes; there are no longer any hostile classes in the country; there is nobody to suppress; hence there is no more need for the state; it must die away. Why then do we not help our Socialist state to die

[6] Stalin, *Problems of Leninism* (Moscow, 1945), pp. 632-38.

away? Why do we not strive to put an end to it? Is it not time to throw out all this rubbish of a state?" . . .

These questions show that those who ask them have conscientiously memorized certain propositions contained in the doctrine of Marx and Engels about the state. But they also show that these comrades have failed to understand the essential meaning of this doctrine; that they have failed to realize in what historical conditions the various propositions of this doctrine were elaborated; and, what is more, that they do not understand present-day international conditions, have overlooked the capitalist encirclement and the dangers it entails for the Socialist country. . . .

Engels' general formula about the destiny of the Socialist state in general cannot be extended to the partial and specific case of the victory of Socialism in one country only, a country which is surrounded by a capitalist world, is subject to the menace of foreign military attack, cannot therefore abstract itself from the international situation, and must have at its disposal a well-trained army, well-organized punitive organs, and a strong intelligence service— consequently, must have its own state, strong enough to defend the conquests of Socialism from foreign attack. . . .

We now have an entirely new, Socialist state, without precedent in history and differing considerably in form and functions from the Socialist state of the first phase.

But development cannot stop there. We are going ahead, towards Communism. Will our state remain in the period of Communism also?

Yes, it will, unless the capitalist encirclement is liquidated, and unless the danger of foreign military attack has disappeared. Naturally, of course, the forms of our state will again change in conformity with the change in the situation at home and abroad.

No, it will not remain and will atrophy if the capitalist encirclement is liquidated and a Socialist encirclement takes its place.

CREATING THE NEW CLASS

A number of theories of Soviet society, of which the best known are those of James Burnham[7] and Milovan Djilas,[8] see

[7] James Burnham, *The Managerial Revolution, or, What Is Happening in the World Now* (New York: The John Day Company, 1941; London: G. P. Putnam's Sons, 1944).

[8] Milovan Djilas, *The New Class* (New York: Frederick A. Praeger, Inc., 1957; London: Thames and Hudson, 1957).

it as dominated by a new privileged class, which is equated to the Soviet "intelligentsia," or at least its managerial and administrative segments. During the 1930s Stalin sought to provide theoretical justification for the existence and special position of this social "stratum," and the following passages are taken from his most pertinent statements on this issue.

1931 [9]

No ruling class has managed without its own intelligentsia. There are no grounds for believing that the working class of the U.S.S.R. can manage without its own industrial and technical intelligentsia. . . . The industrial and technical intelligentsia of the working class will be recruited not only from among those who have passed through the institutions of higher learning, but also from among practical workers in our factories, from the skilled workers, from among the working class cultural forces in the mills, factories and mines. . . . The task is not to discourage these comrades who show initiative, but boldly to promote them to commanding positions; to give them the opportunity to display their organizing abilities and the opportunity to supplement their knowledge; to create suitable conditions for them to work in, not stinting money for this purpose. . . .

1939 [10]

We now have a numerous, new, popular, Socialist intelligentsia, fundamentally different from the old, bourgeois intelligentsia both in composition and in social and political character.

The old theory about the intelligentsia, which taught that it should be treated with distrust and combated, fully applied to the old, pre-revolutionary intelligentsia, which served the landlords and capitalists. This theory is now out-of-date and does not fit our new, Soviet intelligentsia. Our new intelligentsia demands a new theory, a theory teaching the necessity for a cordial attitude towards it, solicitude and respect for it, and cooperation with it in the interests of the working class and the peasantry.

[9] From "New Conditions—New Tasks in Economic Construction," described as a "speech delivered at a conference of business executives," *Problems of Leninism,* pp. 369-70.

[10] From Stalin's report to the Eighteenth Congress, *ibid.,* pp. 639-40.

THE SOCIALIST FATHERLAND

Stalin's policy of "socialism in one country" inevitably raised difficulties for traditional Marxist internationalism. In the 1930s Stalin began to create a new Soviet patriotism, and to nourish it with the national symbols of the Russian past. The following passage, written prophetically ten years before the Nazi invasion, can be regarded as the original manifesto of Soviet patriotism. At the same time it offers a justification for intensified industrialization, with all the sacrifices this entailed, in terms not only of the interests of international communism but also of the national interests of Soviet Russia.[11]

It is sometimes asked whether it is not possible to slow down the tempo a bit, to put a check on the movement. No, comrades it is not possible! The tempo must not be reduced! On the contrary, we must increase it as much as is within our powers and possibilities. This is dictated to us by our obligations to the workers and peasants of the U.S.S.R. This is dictated to us by our obligations to the working class of the whole world.

To slacken the tempo would mean falling behind. And those who fall behind get beaten. But we do not want to be beaten. No, we refuse to be beaten! One feature of the history of old Russia was the continual beatings she suffered for falling behind, for her backwardness. She was beaten by the Mongol khans. She was beaten by the Turkish beys. She was beaten by the Swedish feudal lords. She was beaten by the Polish and Lithuanian gentry. She was beaten by the British and French capitalists. She was beaten by the Japanese barons. All beat her—for her backwardness: for military backwardness, for cultural backwardness, for political backwardness, for industrial backwardness, for agricultural backwardness. She was beaten because to do so was profitable and could be done with impunity. Do you remember the words of the pre-revolutionary poet: "You are poor and abundant, mighty and impotent, Mother Russia." These words of the old poet were well learned by those gentlemen. They beat her, saying: "You are abundant," so one can enrich oneself at your expense. They beat her, saying: "You are poor and impotent," so you can be beaten and plundered with im-

---

[11] From "The Tasks of Building Executives," *ibid.*, pp. 355-56.

punity. Such is the law of the exploiters—to beat the backward and the weak. It is the jungle law of capitalism. You are backward, you are weak—therefore you are wrong; hence, you can be beaten and enslaved. You are mighty—therefore you are right; hence, we must be wary of you.

That is why we must no longer lag behind.

In the past we had no fatherland, nor could we have one. But now that we have overthrown capitalism and power is in the hands of the working class, we have a fatherland, and we will defend its independence. Do you want our Socialist fatherland to be beaten and to lose its independence? If you do not want this you must put an end to its backwardness in the shortest possible time and develop genuine Bolshevik tempo in building up its Socialist system of economy. There is no other way. That is why Lenin said during the October Revolution: "Either perish, or overtake and outstrip the advanced capitalist countries."

We are fifty or a hundred years behind the advanced countries. We must make good this distance in ten years. Either we do it, or they crush us.

STALIN AS WAR LEADER

On July 3, 1941, eleven days after the German invasion, Stalin emerged from seclusion to deliver an unprecedented radio appeal to the Soviet people. He attempted to justify the policies pursued vis-à-vis Hitler, and then went on to develop the themes that were to become the standard ones of World War II: a patriotic war to the death (Marxism-Leninism dwindling almost to extinction), ruthless discipline, and "scorched earth."

The excerpted highlights reveal Stalin's limitations as a popular orator. The contrast with the inspiring ring of a Churchill or the warmth of a Roosevelt are even more obvious in sound recordings of the speech, where the manner and tone of delivery are seen as contrasting grotesquely with the warmth of the opening phrases.[12]

Comrades, citizens, brothers and sisters, men of our Army and Navy! It is to you I am speaking dear friends!

[12] Quoted with permission of the publishers from *Soviet Foreign Policy During the Patriotic War: Documents and Materials*, Vol. I: *June 22, 1941-December 31, 1943*, trans. Andrew Rothstein (London: Hutchinson & Co., n.d.).

The perfidious military attack by Hitlerite Germany on our Motherland, begun on 22 June, is continuing. In spite of the heroic resistance of the Red Army, and although the enemy's finest divisions and finest air force units have already been smashed and have found their graves on the field of battle, the enemy continues to push forward, hurling fresh forces to the front. Hitler's troops have succeeded in capturing Lithuania, a considerable part of Latvia, the western part of Byelorussia and part of Western Ukraine. The Fascist aircraft are extending the range of their operations. . . . Grave danger overhangs our country.

How could it have happened that our glorious Red Army surrendered a number of our cities and districts to the Fascist armies? Is it really true that the German-Fascist troops are invincible, as the braggart Fascist propagandists are ceaselessly trumpeting?

Of course not! History shows that there are no invincible armies and never have been. . . .

As to part of our territory having nevertheless been seized by the German-Fascist troops, this is chiefly due to the fact that the war of Fascist Germany against the U.S.S.R. began under conditions that were favorable for the German forces and unfavorable for the Soviet forces. . . .

It may be asked, how could the Soviet Government have consented to conclude a non-aggression pact with such perfidious people, such monsters, as Hitler and Ribbentrop? Was this not an error on the part of the Soviet Government? Of course not! Non-aggression pacts are pacts of peace between two States. It was such a pact that Germany proposed to us in 1939. Could the Soviet Government have declined such a proposal? I think that not a single peace-loving State could decline a peace agreement with a neighboring State, even though the latter were headed by such monsters and cannibals as Hitler and Ribbentrop. . . .

What did we gain by concluding the non-aggression pact with Germany? We secured our country peace for a year and a half and the possibility of preparing our forces to repulse Fascist Germany, should she risk an attack on our country despite the pact. This was a definite advantage for us and a disadvantage for Fascist Germany. . . .

What is required to put an end to the danger imperilling our country, and what measures must be taken to crush the enemy?

Above all it is essential that our people, Soviet people, should appreciate the full immensity of the danger that threatens our country, and should give up all complacency, casualness and the mentality of peaceful constructive work that was so natural before the war, but which is fatal today, when war has radically changed the whole situation. The enemy is cruel and implacable. He is out to seize our lands watered by the sweat of our brows, to seize our grain and oil secured by the labor of our hands. He is out to restore the rule of the landlords, to restore Tsarism, to destroy the national culture and the national existence as States of the Russians, Ukrainians, Byelorussians, Lithuanians, Latvians, Esthonians, Uzbeks, Tatars, Moldavians, Georgians, Armenians, Azerbaijanians and the other free peoples of the Soviet Union, to Germanize them, to turn them into the slaves of German princes and barons. Thus the issue is one of life and death for the Soviet State, of life and death for the peoples of the U.S.S.R.; the issue is whether the peoples of the Soviet Union shall be free or fall into slavery. The Soviet people must realize this and cease being complacent; they must mobilize themselves and reorganize all their work on a new, wartime footing, where there can be no mercy for the enemy.

Further, there must be no room in our ranks for whimperers and cowards, for panic-mongers and deserters; our people must know no fear in the fight, and must selflessly join our patriotic war of liberation against the Fascist enslavers. Lenin, the great founder of our State, used to say that the chief virtues of Soviet men and women must be courage, valor, fearlessness in struggle, readiness to fight together with the people against the enemies of our country. These splendid virtues of the Bolshevik must become the virtues of millions and millions of the Red Army, of the Red Navy, of all the peoples of the Soviet Union.

All our work must be immediately reorganized on a war footing, everything must be subordinated to the interests of the front and the task of organizing the destruction of the enemy. . . .

The Red Army, Red Navy and all citizens of the Soviet Union must defend every inch of Soviet soil, must fight to the last drop of blood for our towns and villages, must display the daring, initiative and mental alertness characteristic of our people. . . .

We must strengthen the Red Army's rear, subordinating all our work to this end; all our industries must be got to work with greater intensity, to produce more rifles, machine-guns, cartridges, shells, planes; we must organize the guarding of factories, power stations, telephonic and telegraphic communications, and arrange local air-raid protection.

We must wage a ruthless fight against all disorganizers of the rear, deserters, panic-mongers and rumor-mongers; we must exterminate spies, sabotage agents and enemy parachutists, rendering rapid aid in all this to our extermination battalions. We must bear in mind that the enemy is treacherous, cunning, experienced in deception and the dissemination of false rumors. We must reckon with all this, and not fall victims to provocation. All who by their panic-mongering and cowardice hinder the work of defence, no matter who they may be, must be immediately haled before a military tribunal.

In case of a forced retreat of Red Army units, all rolling-stock must be evacuated, the enemy must not be left a single engine, a single railway truck, not a single pound of grain or gallon of fuel. Collective farmers must drive off all their cattle and turn over their grain to the safe keeping of the State authorities, for transportation to the rear. All valuable property, including non-ferrous metals, grain and fuel that cannot be withdrawn, must be destroyed without fail.

In areas occupied by the enemy, partisan units, mounted and foot, must be formed; sabotage groups must be organized to combat enemy units, to foment partisan warfare everywhere, blow up bridges and roads, damage telephone and telegraph lines, set fire to forests, stores and transports. In occupied regions conditions must be made unbearable for the enemy and all his accomplices. They must be hounded and annihilated at every step, and all their measures frustrated.

The war with Fascist Germany cannot be considered an ordinary war. It is not only a war between two armies, it is also a great war of the entire Soviet people against the German-Fascist troops. The aim of this people's war in defence of our country against the Fascist oppressors is not only to eliminate the danger hanging over our country but also to aid all the European peoples groaning under the yoke of German Fascism. In this war of liberation we shall not be alone. In this great war we shall have true allies in the peoples of Europe and America, including the German people which is enslaved by the Hitlerite misrulers. Our war for the freedom of our country will merge with the struggle of the peoples of Europe and America for their independence, for democratic liberties. It will be a united front of the peoples standing for freedom and against enslavement and threats of enslavement by Hitler's Fascist armies. In this connection the historic statement of the British Prime Minister, Mr. Churchill, regarding aid to the Soviet Union, and the declaration of the United States Government signifying readiness to render aid to our country, which can only evoke a feeling of gratitude in the hearts of the peoples of the Soviet Union, are fully comprehensible and symptomatic.

Comrades, our forces are numberless. The overweening enemy will soon learn this to his cost. Side by side with the Red Army many thousands of workers, collective farmers and intellectuals are rising to fight the enemy aggressor. The masses of our people will rise up in their millions. The working people of Moscow and Leningrad have already begun to form People's Guards, many thousands strong, in support of the Red Army. Such People's Guards must be raised in every city which is in danger of enemy invasion; all the working people must be roused to defend with their lives their freedom, their honor and their country in our patriotic war against German Fascism.

In order to ensure the rapid mobilization of all the strength of the peoples of the U.S.S.R., and to repulse the enemy who has treacherously attacked our country, a State Committee of Defence has been formed, and it has now been vested with the entire authority of the State. The State Committee of Defence has begun its work, and calls upon the whole people to rally around the Party of Lenin and Stalin and around the Soviet Government, for self-sacrificing support to the Red Army and Red Navy, for the defeat of the enemy, for victory.

All our strength for the support of our heroic Red Army and our glorious Red Navy!

All the forces of the people for the destruction of the enemy!

Forward to victory!

STALINISM AS USUAL

Stalin not only fought World War II as a patriotic rather than as a class war, but he also encouraged expectations of radical political and economic changes after the war. Once victory was achieved, however, he proceeded to attribute it to the system and policies he had evolved in the 1930s, and to reimpose that system in all its rigors. The following extracts are taken from Stalin's speech in his electorate during the (uncontested) "elections" of 1946.[13]

[13] I. V. Stalin, *Rechi na predvybornykh sobraniiakh izbiratelei stalinskogo izbiratel'nogo okruga goroda Moskvy*, trans. T. H. Rigby and N. Staples (Moscow, 1950), pp. 13-15, 17-19, 22-23.

What, then, are the results of the War? . . .

First and foremost, our victory means that our *social* structure has triumphed, our Soviet social structure has successfully come through its trial in the fires of war and demonstrated its full viability. . . .

Secondly, our victory means that our Soviet *State* structure has triumphed, that our multi-national Soviet State has come through all the trials of war and shown its viability. . . .

Thirdly, our victory means that our Soviet armed forces, our Red Army, has triumphed, that the Red Army has heroically come through all the setbacks of the war, has routed the army of our enemies and emerged from the war victorious. (*Cry from the hall:* "Under the leadership of Comrade Stalin!" *All stand; stormy, uninterrupted applause, passing into an ovation*) . . .

What material potential did the country dispose of before the Second World War? [Gives production details—ED.] . . .

What policy enabled the Communist Party to ensure this material potential in such a short time?

First of all the Soviet policy of industrialization of the country. . . .

Secondly, the policy of collectivization of agriculture. . . .

Now a few words about the work plans of our Communist Party. . . .

So far as plans for a longer term are concerned, the party intends to organize a new upsurge of the economy, which will make it possible for us to something like treble the level of our industry compared with the pre-war period. . . . Only on this condition can we consider that our Motherland will be guaranteed against all accidents. This will require, say, three more five year plans, if not more. But this thing can be done, and we must do it.

BASIS AND SUPERSTRUCTURE

After World War II Stalin made two direct ventures into the domain of theory: a series of comments on the relations between Marxism and the theory of language (1950), and the article Economic Problems of Communism *(1952).*

The following extracts from Stalin's 1950 writings on language are included mainly for their intrinsic importance. It is also instructive, however, to compare them with the earlier examples of his theoretical writing. Despite a heightening of

the ex cathedra *tone, there is a remarkable continuity of style
and approach: the same peculiar blend of clarity and pene-
tration with pedestrian stodginess and dogmatism.*

*A central tenet of Marxism is that the basic determinant of
the institutions and ideas of a society is its economic system
(its "mode of production," which includes class-property relations). The model employed to symbolize this relationship is
that of basis and superstructure. Marx and Engels, however,
left considerable room for dispute as to the precise extent and
nature of the determining influence exercised by the economic
basis, and the importance of feedback from superstructure to
basis. It is obvious that the more one qualifies or limits the
determining influence of the basis, the greater importance
one will tend to assign to political action and the initiating
and decision-making role of the political leader.*

*One distinguished student of Soviet philosophy considers
that the position adopted by Stalin in the present extracts has
"shaken the pillars of Marxist theory itself."* [14] *Before 1950
Soviet theory regarded language as part of the superstructure.
By removing this enormously important aspect of human experience, an aspect that permeates every area of social life,
from the determining influence of the economic basis, and by
placing unprecedented stress on the feedback from superstructure to basis, Stalin was vastly widening the vistas for political
action. This was Stalin's most far-reaching attempt to adapt
the fundamentals of Marxism to his philosophy of "transformism," analysed by Professor Tucker in the next chapter,
and to the realities of totalitarian rule.*[15]

Question. Is it true that language is a superstructure over the basis?
Answer. No, this is not true.

The basis is the economic system of a society at a given stage of
its development. The superstructure consists of the political, legal,
religious, artistic, philosophical views of the society and the political, legal and other institutions corresponding to them.

Every basis has its own superstructure, appropriate to it. The

[14] Gustav A. Wetter, *Dialectical and Historical Materialism: A Historical and
Systematic Survey of Philosophy in the Soviet Union* (London: Routledge &
Kegan Paul, Ltd., 1958; New York: Praeger, 1959), p. 200.

[15] I. Stalin, *Marksizm i voprosy iazykoznaniia*, trans. T. H. Rigby and N. Staples
(Moscow, 1952), pp. 6-10.

basis of the feudal system has its own superstructure, its own political, legal and other views and the institutions appropriate to them; the capitalist basis has its own superstructure, the socialist—its own. If the basis is altered or liquidated, then, following it, its superstructure changes and is liquidated; if a new basis is born, then, following it, there is born the superstructure appropriate to it.

Language, in this respect, fundamentally differs from the superstructure. Let us take, for example, Russian society and the Russian language. In the course of the last 30 years the old capitalist basis has been liquidated in Russia and a new, socialist basis constructed. Correspondingly, the superstructure of the capitalist basis has been liquidated and a new superstructure created, corresponding to the socialist basis. In consequence the old political, legal, and other institutions have been replaced by new, socialist ones. But, in spite of this, the Russian language has remained basically as it was before the October Revolution. . . .

Further. The basis gives rise to the superstructure, but this does not at all mean that it merely reflects the basis, that it is passive, neutral, is indifferent to the fate of its basis, to the fates of classes, to the character of the system. On the contrary, having made its appearance in the world, it becomes the greatest active force, actively assists its basis to take shape and acquire strength, and makes every effort to help the new order to finish off and liquidate the old basis and the old classes. . . .

Language, in this respect, differs fundamentally from the superstructure. Language is not engendered by one basis or another, an old or a new one, within a given society, but by the whole course of history of a society and the history of bases over a period of centuries. It is not created by any one class, but by the whole of society, all the classes of society, by the efforts of hundreds of generations. . . .

It is no secret that the Russian language served Russian capitalism and Russian bourgeois culture up to the October Revolution just as well as it serves the socialist order and the socialist culture of Russian society today. . . .

Further. The superstructure is the product of one epoch, during which a particular economic basis exists and functions. For this reason the life of a superstructure is not long: it is liquidated and disappears with the liquidation and disappearance of the particular basis.

Language, on the contrary, is the product of a whole series of epochs, over the period of which it is formed, enriched, developed, polished. For this reason, language lives incomparably longer than any basis or any superstructure. . . .

And this is quite understandable. Really, why should it be necessary, after every revolution, for the existing structure of a language, its grammatical system and basic vocabulary, to be destroyed and replaced with new ones, as usually happens in the case of a superstructure? Who wants "water," "earth," "mountain," "forest," "fish," "man," "to walk," "to do," "to produce," "to trade," etc., to be called not water, earth, mountain, etc., but something different? Of what use to the revolution is such an upheaval in language? . . .

Finally, there is yet another fundamental distinction between the superstructure and language. The superstructure is not directly tied to production, to the productive activity of man. It is connected to production only obliquely, through the medium of economics, through the medium of the basis. Because of this the superstructure reflects changes in the level of development of the productive forces neither immediately nor directly, but after a change in the basis, through the refraction of these changes in production in changes in the basis. This means that the sphere of action of the superstructure is narrow and limited.

Language, on the contrary, is directly tied to the productive activity of man, and not only to productive activity, but to every other activity of man in all spheres of his work, from production to basis, from basis to superstructure. Because of this, language reflects changes in production immediately and directly, without waiting for changes in the basis. . . .

Therefore:

a) a marxist cannot consider language a superstructure on the basis;

b) to confuse language with the superstructure is to commit a serious error.

3
Robert C. Tucker:
Stalinism and "Transformism"

Due to the totalitarian character of the regime within which Stalin held absolute power, his ideas, attitudes, and personality found expression not only directly in what he himself said and wrote, but also were reflected in all that was said and done in the name of that regime. In particular, the whole sphere of ideology, including science, philosophy, and the arts, was brought more and more into conformity with the mind of Stalin. This process reached its apogee after World War II when new Stalinist dogmas were imposed in one field after another till they covered almost the whole spectrum of intellectual endeavor. The most wide-ranging and penetrating study of this phase is that undertaken by Robert C. Tucker in his The Soviet Political Mind: Studies in Stalinism and Post-Stalin Change. *Analysing the new post-war dogmas in a number of areas of natural and behavioral science, Professor Tucker deduces a unifying logic, which he identifies with the will to transform reality by political means, and which, in turn, he relates to the mentality of Stalin himself. These dogmas thus spelt out for the fields concerned the implications of Stalin's new formulae on the basis and superstructure, developed in relation to linguistics (see chap. 2, "Basis and Superstructure"). It is pertinent to add that the hold of all these dogmas was relaxed after Stalin's death and they were eventually either rejected (e.g., Lysenkoism) or heavily qualified (e.g., Pavlovism).*[1]

[1] From "Stalin and the Uses of Psychology," in Robert C. Tucker, *The Soviet Political Mind: Studies in Stalinism and Post-Stalin Change* (New York. Frederick A. Praeger, Inc.; London and Dunmow: Pall Mall Press, 1963), pp. 92-101, 103-4, 113-14. This article originally appeared in *World Politics*, VIII: 4 (July 1956). Reprinted by permission of the author, the RAND Corporation, Frederick A. Praeger, Inc., and the editors of *World Politics*.

THE WILL TO TRANSFORM

A prominent tendency of Soviet thought during the last years of Stalin's reign was the quest for formulas by which reality could be transformed and remolded to the dictates of the Soviet regime. The idea of transforming things in accordance with a formula was not in itself new; the notion of a revolutionary transformation of capitalist society is as old as Marxism and is rooted particularly deeply in the ways of thought characteristic of Russian Bolshevism. But in Stalin's later years this transformist concept seemed to acquire an obsessive hold upon the regime. Along with it went a mania for bigness and a tendency to apply the various formulas with a dogmatic and indiscriminate rigidity.

During the postwar period, transformism became the reaction of the Stalin regime whenever it was confronted with a genuinely difficult domestic situation that clearly called for remedial measures of some kind. Instead of using the materials at hand and adapting its conduct to the realities present in the situation, it habitually responded with a grandiose project of transformation. In 1949, it came out with the so-called "Stalin Plan for the Transformation of Nature," an immense and costly undertaking of irrigation and afforestation that was to convert rural Russia into a fertile, blooming garden. Closely linked with this was the scheme for transforming the industrial landscape of the country by a series of giant "construction projects of Communism"—canals, dams, and hydroelectric power stations that, it was boasted, would eclipse the best and biggest accomplishments along this line in the United States or any other country. To cite a further example, the Soviet regime, faced with an acute shortage of housing and office space in Moscow, responded with a plan for "transforming the face of the capital." This was to be accomplished by the erection of an ensemble of skyscrapers that would rival those of New York, although, unlike New York, Moscow had abundant space for less ambitious structures, which would have resolved the problem more quickly and economically.

This transformist outlook was reflected in the "biological discussion" of 1948, at which the Michurin-Lysenko doctrines on heredity were accepted officially, with the full authority of the Central Committee of the Communist Party and of Stalin himself. "Michurinism," as these doctrines were called, was a perfect model of transformist thinking. Their founder, the Russian naturalist I. V. Michurin (the "Great Transformer of Nature"), had, it was said, taken a "gigantic step forward" in the further development of Darwinism. Darwin had merely explained the evolutionary process, while "I. V. Michurin made evolution." [2] Michurin, it was said, had discovered laws and methods by which it would be possible to "mold organic forms."

The Michurin-Lysenko teachings are associated with the Lamarckian principle of the inheritance of acquired characteristics. This was the practical crux of the matter. However, the biological issue was only one aspect of an ideological problem. Underlying the controversy over the inheritance of acquired characteristics was a clash between two radically different conceptions of the relationship between the organism and its environment. The Soviet geneticists whose work was based upon the Mendelian school postulated "autogenesis"—evolution under the influence of certain hereditary forces inherent in the organism itself. In this view, the so-called "internal factors of development" assume primary importance, and the role of external environmental conditions in the evolutionary process is reduced to either a "starting mechanism" or a limiting factor. It was essentially this "autogenetic" conception of the organism that Lysenko and his followers, backed by the full authority of the Soviet state, denied and attempted to expunge from Soviet biological thought.

Lysenko was led to this standpoint not by the weight of carefully sifted scientific evidence, but by the imperatives of transformist ideology. Transformist thinking is fundamentally opposed to any conception that endows the object that is to be transformed (in this case, the organism) with developmental autonomy; it must not have spontaneous internal forces for growth or change that the transformer has to reckon with and respect, because that would impose unwanted limits upon the extent to which the object could be transformed from without.

The Michurinist doctrine arose out of this need to conceive the active factor of evolutionary change as residing not in the organism but in controllable conditions of the environment. For transformism, the role of these conditions must be decisive.

If, as this doctrine holds, environmental change is the sole active agent of the evolutionary process, then man's power of control over the environmental conditions of plants and animals enables him to

[2] *The Situation in Biological Science. Proceedings of the Lenin Academy of Agricultural Sciences of the U.S.S.R. Session: July 31-August 7, 1948. Verbatim Report* (1949), p. 274.

direct their evolution according to his needs and purposes. He can then, as the participants of the 1948 session declared in their message to Stalin, "govern the nature of organisms by creating man-controlled conditions of life for plants, animals, micro-organisms." The relationship of this trend of thought to the transformist motivation of the Stalin regime becomes transparently clear. The Michurinist agrobiology, said the final resolution of the session, is "a powerful instrument for the active and planned transformation of living nature." The validity of this claim is debatable. But between 1948 and 1953, Lysenko's theory was an integral component of Stalinism. It provided a rationalization in the biological sphere for Stalinism's effort to impose its dictates upon the world, to transform reality according to its wishes.

THE CULT OF NECESSITY

But while reality can be transformed, the "scientific" laws that govern the transformation are themselves fixed, necessary, and immutable. The will to transform reality was coupled with a vehement denial that there was anything arbitrary, subjective, risky, or unpredictable about the various schemes for transformation that the regime put forward. In this respect, Stalinism made a break with a deep-seated tradition of Bolshevism. The characteristic Bolshevist belief in determinism, its general "denial of accidents," had always previously coexisted with belief in an "indeterminist tendency" with respect to the details of the future, with an allowance for the future's "partial unpredictability." [3]

The mounting obsession with necessity, determinism, and the expulsion of chance from every area of Soviet policy came to a climax in Stalin's last work, *Economic Problems of Socialism in the U.S.S.R.*, published in October, 1952. Until its appearance, it had been an accepted practice for Soviet theorists to maintain that the all-powerful Soviet state, because of its control over every aspect of economic life, could repeal or transform the laws governing its economic operations and create new ones in their stead. But in 1952, Stalin protested vehemently against this idea of the transforming of laws. Those who had spoken in such terms were denounced as economic adventurists whose disdain of "objective regularities" was fraught with great danger.

For what would happen if the Soviet state would regard itself as

---

[3] Nathan Leites, *A Study of Bolshevism* (1953), pp. 67, 84.

competent to create or transform economic laws? It would lead, said Stalin, to "our falling into a realm of chaos and fortuities; we would find ourselves in slavish dependence upon these fortuities; we would deprive ourselves of the possibility not only of understanding, but even of finding our way around in this chaos of fortuities." Therefore, the Soviet state must base its economic policy upon "scientific laws." Scientific laws, in turn, were reflections of "objective processes in nature or society," taking place independently of the will of human beings."

But Stalin simultaneously protested against what he called the "fetishizing" of laws: "It is said that economic laws bear an elemental character, that the effects of these laws are inexorable, that society is powerless before them. This is untrue. This is a fetishizing of laws, the surrender of oneself into slavery to laws. It has been shown that society is not powerless in the face of laws, that society, by perceiving economic laws and relying upon them, can restrict their sphere of action, use them in the interests of society, and 'saddle' them, as happens with the forces of nature and their laws." [4]

There is thus a contradiction in Stalin's doctrine about scientific laws. On the one hand, he insists that Soviet policy must conform with "objective processes taking place independently of the will of human beings." This would eliminate choice and spontaneity from Soviet economic development, which would now be subordinated completely to the dictates of economic necessity. On the other hand, he cannot endure the thought of slavery to laws. He must regard his regime (or himself) as somehow superior to them, able to "saddle" them, subdue them, or "attain mastery over them," as one saddles and subdues the elemental forces of nature. He endeavors to resolve this conflict through the medium of the knowing mind. The function of the mind, he says, is to discover, grasp, study, and apply scientific laws. This intervention of the knowing mind enables him to feel that subordination to objective regularities is different from slavery to them. To settle this point, he cites the statement of Engels (derived from Hegel) equating freedom with "apprehended necessity."

Why was it that Stalin, while set on saddling, subduing, or attaining mastery over the supposedly objective laws of social-economic development, found utterly intolerable the thought of creating, repealing, or transforming them? What explains the enormous

[4] "Ekonomicheskie problemy sotsializma v SSSR," *Voprosy filosofii*, No. 5, 1952, pp. 6, 8, 47.

importance this quasi-verbal distinction evidently had for him? The answer may lie in "externalization," a process by which a person experiences his own thoughts, drives, or standards as operative in the external environment. In Stalin's case this tendency eventually found expression in a legislative attitude toward reality. In other words, what he referred to as "objective scientific laws" were an externalization of his inner policy dictates; they were a projection upon future Soviet history of the formulas for social-economic development generated in his own mind. *His own ideas appeared to him as natural necessities governing the development of society.*

This process of externalization performed for Stalin a double psychological function. First, it stilled any gnawing uncertainty in his own mind about the validity of the formulas and directives that he evolved; there could be nothing arbitrary or capricious about formulas that represented "objective processes taking place independently of the will of human beings." Subjective considerations entered only in the sense that his mind was the first to discover them, as Newton had been the first to discover the law of gravity. Secondly, this mental operation shut off all possible argument. It is reasonable to question a proposition about Soviet policy, even if its author be Stalin, but to question a law of nature is pure impertinence. With this in mind, we can understand how irritated Stalin became at the idea of creating, repealing, or transforming the objective laws of nature and society; such an attitude toward laws was a potential threat to his infallibility, a challenge to his externalized policy dictates. His heavy-handed insistence on the objectivity of all scientific laws, on their independence of the will of human beings, was a means of backing up his own claim to legislate the future course of nature and society. On the other hand, he could easily admit the possibility of "saddling" or "subduing" the laws, because this did not in any way affect their validity but only the manner in which society reacted to the discovery of them. It was his role as Supreme Architect of Communism to discover the laws, and it was the business of Soviet society to study them and put them into effect, and thus to "attain mastery" over them.

These considerations make it plain that the frantic preoccupation with causality, objectivity, and scientific laws that emerged in Soviet theoretical writings and the press during 1952 did not signify a retreat into a more empirical and pragmatic temper. Far from implying adoption of a scientific outlook, in the proper sense of the term, this tendency was part and parcel of the drift of the regime (under the commanding influence of the dictator himself) into the realm of political fantasy and wish-fulfillment. The extreme and at times almost hysterical emphasis upon necessity, iron regularities, objective scientific laws, etc., apparently expressed an imperative need to cover up the arbitrary and willful character of the decisions to transform things to suit the dreams and dictates of the autocracy. The further Stalin went in his schemes for the transformation of nature and society, the more he needed the reassurance that everything was proceeding in accordance with objective laws. The appeal to mechanical causality was a rationalization of rampant adventurism in Stalinist policy.

We have noted Lysenko's expression of scorn for Mendelian genetics because it "resorts" to the theory of probability and relies on "mere statistics." In later years this attitude led to a conscious rejection of any concept of scientific method that ruled out the absolute character of scientific laws. The physicist Bohr, for example, was attacked in 1952 for attempting to transform the law of the preservation of energy from an absolute law of nature into a statistical law that only holds good on the average. The "indeterminacy principle" enunciated by Heisenberg in connection with the quantum theory proved highly bothersome to Soviet philosophers of science, who felt called upon to contend that beneath the superficial appearance of indeterminacy the microparticles of quantum theory must fully conform to a law of "deeper causal determination" of the microprocesses.[5] Especially strongly did they react against the speculation of Western quantum theorists to the effect that the electrons "choose their path," as it were, and thus (metaphorically speaking) possess a certain amount of "free will"; in other words, that there are certain moments when "nature makes a choice." The emotional intensity with which such thoughts were flayed reflects the psycho-ideological motivation of the Stalinist position. To the Stalinist mind it was imperative that nature at all its levels, from the microprocesses to man, be governed by mechanical laws of causality. For only on that condition could it be regarded as infinitely manipulable. The behavior of every single object must be reducible to a rigid, hard-and-fast formula, discovery of which would make it possible to saddle or subdue the object, to gain complete mastery over it, to transform it at will. Therefore, autogenesis was unacceptable. Nothing can behave in spontaneous ways not completely reducible to its objective formula. Everything "subjective" becomes suspect. The endowing of electrons with spon-

[5] B. M. Kedrov, "O materialisticheskom ponimanii Zakonov prirody," *Voprosy filosofii*, No. 6, 1952, pp. 69, 71.

taneity was similar to the endowing of living organisms with developmental and mutational tendencies inherent in their genes. In either case the ideal of total control and transformability would be jeopardized. Here was an outlook that might fairly be described as the projection of totalitarianism upon nature.

THE FORMULA FOR MAN

Inevitably, the postulates of transformism and mechanical causality penetrated the areas of Soviet thought concerned with· the behavior of man. There were also special reasons for this. The most difficult problem faced by the Stalin regime in the postwar years was the profound passivity of the Soviet populace, its failure to respond positively to the goals set before it.

Stalin evidently decided that the problem could be solved, or at least greatly alleviated, by a massive propaganda effort coupled with improved controls over an intermediate element—the artists and writers—whose work in the service of the goals of the state would in turn influence the public in the required ways. This was one impulse behind "Zhdanovism," the drive that started in the summer of 1946 to enlist and organize the creative intelligentsia of the Soviet Union as a corps of conscious instruments of state policy, as missionaries of patriotic enthusiasm among the dispirited multitude of the Russian people. The attempt to elicit popular enthusiasm by means of a propaganda campaign continued through the postwar years, but with little apparent success. The whole undertaking was an example of Stalinism's characteristic overevaluation of the potentialities of propaganda.

As indicated earlier, the typical reaction of the Stalin regime to a situation in which certain forces in the environment were proving recalcitrant to its goals was not to re-examine the goals, but to search for a formula by which it could transform or remold the forces and thereby overcome their recalcitrance. If the material at hand was showing itself perverse to the dictates of the regime, then some way had to be found to conquer its perversity. The dictates themselves were righteous and unalterable; their frustration only evoked redoubled insistence upon their realization. In the case in question, the regime was faced with persistent popular apathy and passive resistance to its control in various sections of Soviet society, especially the peasantry. People were not responding in the expected way to the techniques of political education and indoctrination. This led the Stalinist mind to seek a formula for making people respond properly. If Russians were failing to respond to the goals set before them, then something was the matter with the Russians and with the means employed to elicit their response. Their minds had to be remolded to the point where inner acceptance of the Soviet ideology and all the behavior patterns it imposed would come as a matter of course. But for mind control to become a reality, it had to be based upon scientific bedrock. What was required was a *formula for man.*

By 1949, when the need for a new formula in terms of which human nature could be scientifically explained and "saddled" had become more or less obvious, Stalin found in the Michurin-Lysenko doctrines a theory of the transformation of organisms on the biological level. Could he not draw in some fashion upon these doctrines for the purpose of constructing a more perfect science of man? We know that he tended to employ the biological analogy in his sociological thinking. In his essay on "Dialectical and Historical Materialism" published in 1938 as a chapter of the *Short Course,* he had written that the science of society "can become as precise a science as, let us say, biology, and capable of making use of the laws of development of society for practical purposes." [6] Lysenko, with Stalin's blessing, had become the reigning authority of a new biology which boasted of its ability to "expel fortuities" from this area of knowledge. If Michurinism could produce new species of plants and animals, might it not serve in the hands of the all-powerful Soviet state as a means of eventually creating a new species of "Soviet man"?

Actually, a "Michurinism for man" was germinating during the aftermath of the genetics controversy of 1948, but it did not come forth as a Soviet version of eugenics. It was a transference to man not of the specific biological concepts and techniques of Michurinism, but of its basic underlying ways of thought, of its general theory of the relationship between the organism and the environment. In his search for a counterpart of Michurin in the field of psychology, for a Russian who could qualify as the "great transformer of human nature," Stalin rediscovered Pavlov. *The formula for man was the conditioned reflex.*

This rediscovery heralded a Pavlovian revolution in the Soviet behavioral sciences. The principle of the conditioned reflex was made the basis of a new Soviet concept of man. According to this

[6] *History of the Communist Party of the Soviet Union (Bolshevik): Short Course* (1945), pp. 114-115.

concept, man is a reactive mechanism whose behavior, including all the higher mental processes, can be exhaustively understood through a knowledge of the laws of conditioning, and can be controlled through application of this knowledge. The new movement began in 1949, and continued with ever-increasing momentum during 1950, 1951, and 1952. From the fields of physiology and medicine, where it took its rise, it radiated out into numerous adjacent areas of science, including psychiatry, pedagogy, and psychology.

It must be emphasized once again that the motivating springs of this movement were not scientific but political, not intellectual in the proper sense but psycho-ideological. That is, the neo-Pavlovian movement did not grow spontaneously out of the scientific investigations of Soviet physiologists, pathologists, and psychologists working independently at their respective problems. It was, on the contrary, imposed upon them from above by political authorities whose interest in the matter was nonscientific. According to Academician K. Bykov, who played a part in the Pavlovian revolution similar to that of Lysenko in genetics, the whole development took place "under the directing influence of the Party" and was inspired by Stalin personally: "The initiator of the events that have elevated the teachings of Pavlov in our country, the initiator of the creation of the most favorable conditions for the development of Soviet physiology for the benefit of the people is the brilliant architect of Soviet culture—Joseph Vissarionovich Stalin. We are indebted to Comrade Stalin for the victory of the Pavlovian cause in our country and for the creative upsurge we now observe in the development of this most important field of contemporary natural science." [7] There appears to be no reason to doubt the testimony of Bykov on this crucial point.

The relationship of the Pavlovian doctrine to the transformist goals of the Soviet regime and to the Michurinist ideology was made explicit by Bykov and Ivanov-Smolensky. Pavlov, declared the latter, had aspired not only to study but also to *master* the phenomena being studied, to direct them, command them, change them in the required directions. Through a knowledge of the laws of conditioning combined with control over the environment, behavior could be conditioned in whatever ways were considered desirable. In addition, the conditioned connections, repeated for a number of generations, could "by heredity turn into unconditioned ones." The organic relationship between Michurinism and Pavlovianism in the minds of the Soviet proponents of these doctrines was reflected in

[7] *Pravda,* April 19, 1952.

the later appearance in Soviet writings of a new hyphenated expression: the "Michurin-Pavlov biology." According to this conception, the common basic principle of the two doctrines was the "law of the unity of organism and environment." The difference between them related only to the spheres of application of the basic principle. Michurinism applied it to agriculture, while Pavlovianism applied it to physiology, psychology, and medicine.

At this point it may be useful to summarize briefly the argument of the foregoing pages. I have suggested that the movement initiated by Stalin to reconstruct Soviet psychology marked a decline of the optimistic conception of man that had officially prevailed in the U.S.S.R. since the early 1930's. This in turn was an indirect reflection of the fact that millions of Russians, especially under the impact of their experiences during and after World War II, showed tendencies to deviate radically from the norm of Soviet selfhood, which, according to the optimistic conception, they should have naturally assimilated as a result of their education and spontaneous personality development. In the face of this disturbing fact, Stalin resorted to the peculiar mode of coming to terms with perverse situations that we have termed "transformism." In the Pavlovian model of personality he found a formula that seemed to place human nature in the arbitrary power of a state-controlled educational environment. Emptied of all inner springs of character and conduct, man appeared in this model as a passive plaything of determining influences from without, particularly influences of a social character brought to bear through the medium of language. By mastering the "objective scientific laws" of the language-conditioning process, the state could—theoretically—bring about the "directed alteration of psychic processes," i.e., it could transform the minds of its citizens, mold them in the Soviet personality image. The crowning concept of this theoretical edifice was the second signal system. In the Stalin-Pavlov model of man, the second signal system is the mechanism of mentality. Consciousness is the distinctive capacity of human beings to respond to and regulate their behavior by verbal signals. Man is basically a signal-receiving animal. And since it is the state that calls the signals, an appropriate name for this theoretical new species of Soviet humanity would be "state-directed man."

THE WORLD LOOKS AT STALIN

4

Doing Business
with Stalin

What qualities of character and personality did Stalin manifest in face-to-face situations? What was his personal appearance? In going about the business of his day-to-day life, what kinds of relationship did he seek to establish, what were his preferred procedures, what strengths and weaknesses did he reveal? This chapter attempts to throw light on these questions by recording the observations and reactions of persons who had experience in dealing with Stalin, including fellow-revolutionaries and colleagues as well as foreign journalists and statesmen.

LENIN: "A SPLENDID GEORGIAN"

It was in 1912-13 that Stalin first entered the national *leadership of the Bolshevik party, which Lenin was then engaged in separating definitively from the rest of the Russian Social-Democratic Party. The following remark made by Lenin toward the end of a letter to the writer Maxim Gorki, then a prominent member of the Russian socialist movement, is his earliest known evaluation of his new lieutenant. The letter bears witness both to Stalin's relative obscurity in the movement and to Lenin's enthusiastic but patronizing attitude toward him.*[1]

[1] From Lenin's letter to Gorki, written from Cracow in February 1913, in *V. I. Lenin i A. M. Gorkii: Pis'ma, vospominaniia, dokumenty,* 2nd ed. (Moscow, 1961), p. 98.

On the question of nationalism I am in complete agreement with you that we have to pay more serious attention to it. We've got a splendid Georgian here who has settled down to write a big article for *Prosveshchenie*,[2] bringing together *all* the Austrian and other material. We will really put our backs into this.

"CERTAIN PERSONAL TRAITS"

Even in the prerevolutionary period Stalin had earned a reputation for unfortunate personal characteristics that bore on his suitability as a revolutionary leader or colleague. In March 1917, after Stalin's return from Siberia to Saint Petersburg, the Russian Bureau of the Bolshevik Central Committee gave "certain personal traits" as their reason for refusing to co-opt him as a full voting member. In April, after the return of Lenin, for whom Stalin's toughness and practical abilities far outweighed any personal defects, Stalin was to be admitted into the Bolshevik inner leadership. By the time Lenin himself realized that Stalin's defects of character might "acquire decisive significance" (see below, "Lenin: 'Let's Get Rid of Him'"), it proved too late to correct his error.[3]

The following document was made public in 1963.

Concerning Stalin it was submitted that he was a Central Committee Agent in 1912 and that it would therefore be desirable to have him in the Bureau of the Central Committee; but in view of certain personal traits characteristic of him the Bureau of the Central Committee expressed itself in favor of asking him to attend in a consultative capacity.

SUKHANOV: "A GRAY BLUR"

There is general agreement that Stalin's rise was not due to his personal impact exercised on a public level, and the medi-

---

[2] A Russian Marxist theoretical journal. The article referred to was Stalin's "Marxism and the National Question."

[3] From the Protocols of the Bureau of the (Bolshevik) Central Committee, quoted by A. V. Snegov, "Neskol'ko stranits iz istorii partii," *Voprosy Istorii KPSS*, No. 2, 1963, p. 19.

*ocrity of his public performances was often noted by his con-
temporaries. Here is the impression he made on a prominent
participant in and historian of the revolutionary events of
1917.*[4]

At this time Stalin appeared in the Ex. Com.[5] for the Bolsheviks, in addition to Kamenev. This man was one of the central
figures of the Bolshevik Party and perhaps one of the few individuals who held (and hold to this day) the fate of the revolution
and of the State in their hands. Why this is so I shall not undertake
to say: 'influence' in these exalted and irresponsible spheres, remote
from the people and alien to publicity, is so capricious. But at any
rate Stalin's role is bound to be perplexing. The Bolshevik Party,
in spite of the low level of its 'officers' corps,' had a whole series of
most massive figures and able leaders among its 'generals.' Stalin,
however, during his modest activity in the Ex. Com. produced—
and not only on me—the impression of a gray blur, looming up
now and then dimly and not leaving any trace. There is really
nothing more to be said about him.

TROTSKY: "VULGARITY AND ANIMOSITY"

*Working with Stalin after the Bolshevik seizure of power,
the cosmopolitan, émigré leaders of the party also began to
realize that the "gray blur" possessed "certain personal traits."
The following is Trotsky's account of an early encounter.*[6]

When I arrived in Petrograd at the beginning of May [1917—
ED.], I hardly remembered Stalin's name. I probably ran across it
in the Bolshevik press, signed to articles which hardly held my
attention. . . . After the Revolution the first session of the Bol-

[4] N. N. Sukhanov, *The Russian Revolution 1917*, trans. J. Carmichael (London:
Oxford University Press, 1955), pp. 229-30. Reprinted by permission of the
publishers and translator.

[5] The Executive Committee of the Petrograd Soviet.

[6] Leon Trotski, *Stalin: An Appraisal of the Man and His Influence*, ed. and
trans. Charles Malamuth (London: Hollis and Carter, Ltd., 1947), pp. 242-44.
Reprinted by permission of Hollis & Carter, Ltd., London.

shevik Government took place in Smolny, in Lenin's office, where an unpainted wooden partition segregated the cubbyhole of the telephone girl and the typist. Stalin and I were the first to arrive. From behind the partition we heard the thick basso of Dybenko. He was speaking by telephone with Finland, and the conversation had a rather tender character. The twenty-nine-year-old, black-bearded sailor, a jolly and self-confident giant, had recently become intimate with Alexandra Kollontai, a woman of aristocratic antecedents who knew a half dozen foreign languages and was approaching her forty-sixth year. In certain circles of the Party there was undoubtedly a good deal of gossip about this. Stalin, with whom until then I had not carried on a personal conversation, came up to me with a kind of unexpected jauntiness and, pointing with his shoulder toward the partition, said, smirking: "That's he with Kollontai, with Kollontai!" His gestures and his laughter seemed to me out of place and unendurably vulgar, especially on that occasion and in that place. I don't remember whether I simply said nothing, turning my eyes away, or answered drily, "That's their affair." But Stalin sensed that he had made a mistake. His face changed, and in his yellow eyes appeared the same glint of animosity that I had noticed in Vienna.[7] From that time on he never again attempted to engage me in conversation on personal themes.

TROTSKY: STALIN
AS CIVIL WAR LEADER

Stalin's role in the military side of the Civil War was a comparatively minor one, but it provided the occasion for his first serious conflict with Trotsky, who was supreme organizer and leader of the Red Army. In 1918 a group of Bolshevik leaders at Tsaritsyn, on the Southern Front, including some of Stalin's old comrades from the Caucasus attempted to resist certain of Trotsky's basic military policies, and Stalin took advantage of this to weld them into a group of personal supporters. In the following passage Trotsky refers to this incident, and also evaluates Stalin's qualities and shortcomings as a military leader.[8]

[7] Trotsky is referring here to his first meeting with Stalin, in 1913, when Stalin was working on his article "Marxism and the National Question."

[8] Trotski, *op. cit.,* pp. 270-71.

There were two aspects to military work in the epoch of the Civil War. One was to select the necessary workers, to make proper disposition of them, to establish the necessary supervision over the commanding staff, to extirpate the suspects, to exert pressure, to punish. All of these activities of the administrative machine suited Stalin's talents to perfection. But there was also another side, which had to do with the necessity of improvising an Army out of human raw material, appealing to the hearts of the soldiers and the commanders, arousing their better selves, and inspiring them with confidence in the new leadership. Of this Stalin was utterly incapable. It is impossible, for example, to imagine Stalin appearing under the open sky before a regiment; for that he did not have any qualifications at all. He never addressed himself to the troops with written appeals, evidently not trusting his own seminarist rhetoric. His influence at those sectors of the front where he worked was not significant. It remained impersonal, bureaucratic and policemanlike.

I remember during the Civil War asking a member of the Central Committee, Serebryakov, who at that time was working with Stalin in the Revolutionary Council of War of the Southern Front, whether he could not manage without Stalin for the sake of economizing forces? Serebryakov replied: "No, I cannot exert pressure like Stalin. It is not my specialty." The ability to "exert pressure" was what Lenin prized so highly in Stalin. The more the state machine for "exerting pressure" gained momentum and the further the spirit of the revolution was removed from this machine, the more confident Stalin felt. . . .

Conflicts between the lower and higher orders are in the nature of things. The army is almost always dissatisfied with the front, the front is always agitating against the General Staff, especially when things do not go very happily. What characterized Stalin is that he systematically exploited these frictions and developed them into bitter feuds. Drawing his collaborators into dangerous conflicts, Stalin thereby welded them together and placed them in dependence upon himself. Twice he was recalled from the front by direct order of the Central Committee. But at each new turn of events he was again sent out. Notwithstanding repeated opportunities, he acquired no prestige in the Army. However, those military collaborators who were under his command, once having been drawn into the struggle against the Center, remained in the future closely connected with him. The Tsaritsyn group became the nucleus of the Stalinist faction.

LENIN: "LET'S GET RID OF HIM"

In the last year or so of his life, the invalid Lenin became increasingly concerned about the future of his revolution. Bureaucratization, corruption, nationalism, and the personal failings of his lieutenants, which had seemed secondary matters so long as he was at the helm, he now saw as threatening the prospects and indeed the very existence of the new society. Meanwhile, Lenin personally experienced for the first time the unscrupulousness and vindictiveness of Stalin when crossed.[9] In December 1922 and January 1923 he dictated, in what became known as "Lenin's Testament," his comments on a number of leaders, including Stalin, who, he said, should be shifted from the post of Secretary-General. Although the "testament" later became well known in the higher circles of the party, Stalin was enabled by a combination of skill, luck, and the scruples of his opponents to weather its effects and retain control of the party machine.[10]

(December 24, 1922)

Comrade Stalin, having become General Secretary, has concentrated limitless power in his hands, and I am not certain that he will always be careful enough in the use of this power.

(Addendum January 4, 1923)

Stalin is too rough,[11] and this shortcoming, while completely tolerable in relations among us communists, becomes intolerable in the post of General Secretary. Therefore I propose to the comrades to think over the means of transferring Stalin from this post and appointing to it some other person who is superior to Stalin only in one respect, namely, in being more tolerant, more loyal, more polite and more attentive to comrades, less capricious, and so on. This circumstance may seem an insignificant trifle. But I think that, from the point of view of preventing a split and from the point of view

[9] See Deutscher, *Stalin: A Political Biography* (English ed.), pp. 244-55.

[10] V. I. Lenin, *Polnoe sobranie sochinenii,* 5th ed., XLV (Moscow, 1964), pp. 345-46.

[11] The Russian word, *grub,* can also mean "rude" or "crude," and is stronger than its English equivalents.

of what I have written above about the relations between Stalin and Trotsky, it is not a trifle, or it is the kind of trifle that is capable of acquiring decisive significance.

BARMINE: "THE BOSS"

During the 1920s Stalin gradually established his domi-nance over the Soviet leadership through his manipulation of the party machine. In the following passage Alexander Barmine, who was a junior official at the time and who sub-sequently broke with the Soviet government, tells how Stalin appeared from below to a perceptive member of his staff.[12]

He was about to leave the imposing Hall of St. George, where the Congress was held, when I first saw him. As he approached the head of the stairway, wearing a military greatcoat over his semi-military tunic and boots, an obscure young clerk employed at the Comintern office stopped him and asked him a question. I was sit-ting on a near-by bench, smoking, idly watching the delegates go out. The Comintern clerk was undersized, and, as frequently is true of people of very short stature, he was inordinately active. Although Stalin himself is not above five feet six, the little clerk hardly came up to his shoulders. Stalin towered over him, nodding occasionally or dropping a word, listening impassively. The little fellow hopped around, tugging at Stalin's sleeve, lapel, or button, talking inces-santly and with what would be to me an irritating ardor, as though burning up with more enthusiasm than he had room to contain. What held my attention and made me remember the scene was Stalin's amazing patience. He struck me as an ideal listener. He was on the verge of departing, had one foot on the edge of the stairs, yet he stood there for almost an hour, calm, unhurried, at-tentive, as though he had all the time in the world to give to this agitated little clerk. There was something monumental about his manner.

That first impression remained always in my memory, an impres-sion of stability and patient force. Patience is a rare trait in men of action. It is not usually found in conjunction with "capriciousness,"

[12] From Alexander Barmine, *One Who Survived: The Life Story of a Russian Under the Soviets*, pp. 257-60. Copyright 1945 by Alexander Barmine. Reprinted by permission of G. P. Putman's Sons.

"disloyalty," "rudeness," and a dangerous thirst for power—the four traits with which Lenin, in his deathbed letter to the Party, his *Testament,* characterized Stalin. That rare combination is the principal key to his character. . . .

At public meetings Stalin never sits in the center, but always at the side or back. When he rises he waves away the applause as though it were an annoyance, although obviously he enjoys the tribute, and the life of a Russian orator who got more applause than he did would not be worth two cents. At state receptions, when playing the gracious host to *Stakhanovites,* Heroes of Labor, Arctic flyers, etc., he behaves with studied simplicity—an unassuming friend to all, especially the diffident provincials. When entertaining at his home with his phonograph, Stalin himself selects the records and places them on the disk. Although he never dances, he urges others to dance, overcoming their shyness in the presence of the leader. He even goes to the trouble of finding a likely partner for a young man.

At party sessions or business conferences Stalin usually listens quietly, smoking his pipe or a cigarette. While listening he is jotting aimless curlicues on the pad before him. . . .

Stalin is widely regarded as a "man of mystery." . . . But to us who worked under him, he did not seem mysterious; he seemed a man with a sense of inferiority which made him touchy, vindictive, and suspicious. He seemed a ruthless and unscrupulous man, concentrated on problems of personal power, and, partly for that reason, partly because of natural limitations, lacking in statesman-like vision. We knew him as a slow and plodding thinker, cautious and suspicious. . . .

Stalin speaks in a slow monotone which is tiresome to the ear. At Politburo and Central Committee meetings during Lenin's lifetime, both before and after the Revolution, he used to sit apart, sulky and silent, unable to participate in the rapid fire of ideas and seeming to despise the whole thing as idle chatter.

FISCHER: "UNSENTIMENTAL, STEEL-WILLED, UNSCRUPULOUS, AND IRRESISTIBLE"

The American "labor delegation" which interviewed Stalin in 1927 included the journalist Louis Fischer, who later became well known for his writings on Soviet Russia. Fischer's acutely observed impressions of Stalin's appearance, manner, and personality offer an invaluable record of the Secretary-General on the verge of absolute power.[13]

We entered Stalin's large reception room at one o'clock in the afternoon. We sat with Stalin until seven-fifteen in the evening. During all this time Stalin never once left the room. He never once sent out a message or received a message. There was no telephone in the room. Here was the man at the helm of Soviet Russia. All threads ended in his hand. Yet he had deliberately cut himself off from everything and everybody for almost an entire working day. He had so organized his work that he could devote himself exclusively to his visitors. This concentration is characteristic of Stalin.

Twice during our prolonged stay, on instructions previously issued, a typical Russian working woman brought in cheese, sausage, and caviar sandwiches and a large steaming samovar—the word means 'self-cooker'—with tumblers for tea with lemon. This woman was the only person to enter the room.

When we arrived Stalin gave each of us a sharp, energetic handshake and invited us to occupy chairs around a long table covered with green felt cloth. He wore high black leather boots, and a civilian khaki suit the trousers of which were stuffed into his boots below the knees. His body is solid but not fat and he moves quickly and softly. If I had seen him without knowing who he was, he would never have impressed me. He looked like any one of a million Soviet working men.

Stalin sat at the head of the table. I sat first on his left making bad pencil sketches of his head and keeping notes which I now have before me. My notes read, 'Deep pock marks over his face,' 'crafty eyes,' 'low forehead,' 'thick bushy black hair,' 'ugly, short, black and gold teeth when smiles.' He smiled little. He was busy. But at conferences and public meetings, during periods of relaxation, I had seen him laugh uproariously.

Trotzky waves the magic wand of a magnetic personality and captures his interlocutor. Stalin does not. But as he talked to us hour after hour my respect for his strength, will, and faith grew. He built up this impression as he built up his political position—slowly, methodically, brick by brick. Nothing Stalin said through-

---

[13] From Louis Fischer, *Men and Politics: An Autobiography* (New York: Duell, Sloan and Pearce, Inc.; London: Jonathan Cape, 1941), pp. 89-91. Reprinted by permission.

out the interview was brilliant. He was pedestrian, solid and simple. His statements interested professors of economy and would have been intelligible to factory hands. The questions had been submitted to him in advance, and he probably prepared the answers in advance. Sometimes he did not grasp the meaning of the question, and rambled before he reached its pith, but finally he did get to the point. His replies were always long and thorough. His mentality lacked the witty epigram or the remark with insight which can light up a whole field of thought. He ploughed long and deep. His complete composure, the complete absence of nerves, and his calm voice reflected inner power. One could see that he might be a man of iron.

The questions posed to Stalin dealt with theoretical Marxism, Leninism, and imperialism. He would not allow himself to be drawn into a discussion of his differences with Trotzky. That was not a subject for a Communist leader to discuss with non-Communists. He did say this: Lenin 'proved that it was possible to construct a complete socialist society in a land of the dictatorship of the proletariat encircled by imperialist states.' . . .

More questions to Stalin. Is there personal incentive in Russia? Does the American Communist party get its orders and money from Moscow? He said it might under certain circumstances. Must a Communist be an atheist? While he was answering this question the chiming of bells in a church across the street drowned out his voice. He smiled and we laughed. (In later years, church bells were silenced by decree.) Yes, a Communist must be an atheist.

These questions and more questions were put to Stalin. After three hours one could see delegates sitting on the edges of their chairs, and Jerome Davis was getting ready to say something like, 'Thank you, Mr. Stalin, for your kindness in granting us so much of your time,' but Stalin never gave him a chance. Finally, at the end of four hours, Davis did deliver his speech. But Stalin said, 'No, no. I have answered your questions. Now you must answer mine.' And for two and a quarter hours he asked questions and the Americans answered. He inquired why so few American workers belong to trade unions, whether unemployment insurance existed in America as in Russia, why there was no labor party in the United States, and why the American government had not yet recognized Soviet Russia. That was all. He gave each one a second bone-crushing handshake and we left. I felt that Stalin was typical of many Bolsheviks—unsentimental, steel-willed, unscrupulous, and irresistible.

DAVIES: "KINDLY AND WISE"

When he wished, Stalin was capable of manifesting a simple, folksy charm which some of his interlocutors found completely disarming. This was the experience of Joseph E. Davies, United States Ambassador to Moscow, 1936-38, who recorded in a letter to his daughter his impressions of an unexpected meeting with Stalin. Note that this meeting occurred in the midst of the Yezhovshchina, *when Stalin was engaged in exterminating dozens of his old comrades and in sentencing millions of innocent Soviet citizens to the horrors of forced labor.*[14]

Well, after I had left President Kalinin's office and gone to the Premier's apartment—and within a very few minutes after sitting down at the desk—I was perfectly amazed and almost struck dumb with surprise to see the far-end door of the room open and Stalin come in alone. I had not the remotest idea it was going to happen. In the first place, he is not the head of the state, and it is his purpose and theirs, apparently, to keep him apart from the state, and, as you know, no diplomat ever sees him officially or otherwise in a personal way. In fact, he avoids any such meeting. So closely has he been shielded from the public that it has almost become a historical event when he receives any foreigner.

Well, when he came in, of course, I stood up and approached him. He greeted me cordially with a smile and with great simplicity, but also with a real dignity. He gives the impression of a strong mind which is composed and wise. His brown eye is exceedingly kindly and gentle. A child would like to sit in his lap and a dog would sidle up to him. It is difficult to associate his personality and this impression of kindness and gentle simplicity with what has occurred here in connection with these purges and shootings of the Red Army generals, and so forth. His friends say, and Ambassador Troyanovsky assures me, that it had to be done to protect themselves against Germany—and that some day the outside world will know "their side."

We sat down at the table and with an interpreter talked for two

[14] Joseph E. Davies, *Mission to Moscow* (New York: Simon and Schuster, Inc., 1941; London: Victor Gollancz Limited, 1943), pp. 230-31. Reprinted by permission of Simon and Schuster, Inc. and Laurence Pollinger Limited.

hours. Of course, I cannot write here what we talked about, for that is only for the President, the Secretary of State, and our government, but I can say that the discussion ranged over the whole field of economy, industrial conditions in Russia, problems of the United States, personality of President Roosevelt, the European situation, the situation in the Far East—all in a very general way. It was really an intellectual feast, which we all seemed to enjoy. Throughout it we joked and laughed at times. He has a sly humour. He has a very great mentality. It is sharp, shrewd, and, above all things else, wise, at least so it would appear to me. If you can picture a personality that is exactly opposite to what the most rabid anti-Stalinist anywhere could conceive, then you might picture this man. The conditions that I know to exist here and his personality are just as far apart as the poles. The explanation, of course, may be found in the fact that men will do for religion or for a cause things that they would never do otherwise. It is the fanaticism of the world that has brought the greatest cruelties.

DURANTY: "CHILLED STEEL"

Walter Duranty, an American journalist who spent many years in the Soviet Union, demurs from the foregoing evaluation, and draws attention to Stalin's stress on the power of human will.[15]

Former Ambassador Davies has written in a letter to his daughter his impressions of Stalin as follows: "His brown eye is exceedingly kind and gentle. A child would like to sit on his knee." . . . With all deference to Mr. Davies, it is difficult to accept that "kind and gentle brown eye." In my first interview with Stalin I asked him an innocent question: "Do you believe in luck?" My purpose was to put some human interest in what seemed a rather drab interview, but I got an unexpected result. That "kind and gentle" eye was hard as chilled steel. He banged his fist on the desk and said: "What do you think I am . . . an old Georgian granny to believe in gods and devils? I'm a Bolshevik and believe in none of that nonsense."

[15] Walter Duranty, *Stalin & Co.: The Men Who Run Russia* (New York: William Sloane Associates, Inc., 1949), pp. 47-48. Copyright © 1949 by Walter Duranty. Reprinted by permission of the publisher.

I hastened to explain that I meant nothing personal but was thinking of Napoleon who believed in his star and Cromwell who always said—and it happened so—that his greatest successes occurred on his own birthday . . . in short, belief in luck. Stalin smiled a trifle coldly and accepted my apology and said: "I see what you mean, but the answer is still no. I believe in one thing only, the power of the human will." A fair and sturdy statement, but hardly that of a man whose brown eyes are kindly or on whose knee a child would like to climb.

He said another thing: "Lenin differed from the rest of us by his clear Marxist brain and his unfaltering will." One might underline the last two words, although Stalin didn't stress them. Then he added: "Lenin from the outset favored a hard-boiled policy and picked men who could stick it out and endure."

HILGER: "THE COMPLEAT DECISION-MAKER"

Gustav Hilger, an experienced and perceptive member of the German Embassy staff, acted as interpreter at the negotiations which led to the Hitler-Stalin pact of 1939. In the following passage he brings together the two facets of Stalin noted by Davies and Duranty, and illustrates Stalin's mastery of technical detail, his capacity for apt and prompt decision, and his dominance of the Soviet decision-making establishment.[16]

Stalin's behavior was simple and unpretentious, an attitude that was just as much a part of his discussion tactics as the paternal benevolence with which he knew how to win his opponents and make them less vigilant. But it was interesting to observe the swiftness with which the jovial friendliness of Stalin's attitude toward von Ribbentrop or the jocular and kind manner in which he dealt

[16] From Gustav Hilger and Alfred G. Meyer, *The Incompatible Allies: A Memoir-History of German-Soviet Relations 1918-1941* (New York: The Macmillan Company, 1953), pp. 301-3. Copyright 1953 by The Macmillan Company. Reprinted by permission of The Macmillan Company.

with one of his junior assistants turned into icy coldness when he rapped out short orders or asked some pertinent question.

I have seen with my own eyes the submissive attitude of the Red Army's chief of staff, General Boris Shaposhnikov, when Stalin would converse with him. I remember the officious and obedient manner in which people's commissars like Tevosyan would rise from their seats like schoolboys when Stalin would deign to ask them a question. In all the conferences at which I saw Stalin, Molotov was the only subordinate who would talk to his chief as one comrade to another. Yet one could clearly sense how he looked up to him, and how lucky he felt to be privileged to serve him. . . .

In meetings with Stalin he frequently surprised us by the extent of his knowledge in technical questions that were being debated, and by the assurance with which he made decisions. Even in matters of style, when the problem was to find the correct words for a diplomatic document or an official communiqué, he would act with assurance and display great judgment and tact. I remember handing him the draft of the joint communiqué explaining the Soviet move into Poland, which I had translated into Russian. Stalin glanced at it quickly, then took a pencil and asked the ambassador's permission to make a few changes in the text. He did so in a matter of minutes, without once consulting Molotov, who sat beside him; then he handed me the amended text, asking me to translate it into German for the ambassador. I whispered to Count Schulenburg [the German Ambassador—Ed.], "He has improved it tremendously." Indeed, Stalin's text was a much more "diplomatic" announcement of the move we intended to bring to public knowledge. "The old Romans," Stalin said, turning to me, "did not go into battle naked, but covered themselves with shields. Today correctly worded political communiqués play the role of such shields." . . .

I was similarly impressed by Stalin's technical knowledge when, for instance, he chaired a meeting of German and Russian experts discussing the ordnance specifications of the turrets for a cruiser which Germany was to deliver to the Soviet Union, or when the German trade delegation discussed with Stalin the volume and character of deliveries to be made by both countries. Without Stalin's express permission it was impossible to obtain any Soviet agreement to sell us certain raw materials; but once his permission had been given it was tantamount to an order which was faithfully executed.

RIBBENTROP: "UNUSUAL STATURE"

Hitler's Foreign Minister, Joachim von Ribbentrop, concurred in Hilger's high estimation of Stalin's political talents and power.[17]

From the moment of meeting Stalin had impressed me as a man of unusual stature. His sober, almost dry and yet so apt way of expressing himself, the hardness and yet generosity of his bargaining, showed that he bore his name not without good reason. The course which our discussion and conversation took gave me a clear idea of the strength and power of this man, whose very movement of a finger was law in the remotest village of this vast country of Russia, of this man who had succeeded in welding together the 200 million inhabitants of his empire more firmly than the Czar had ever been able to do.

HITLER: "HALF BEAST, HALF GIANT"

Hitler's recorded private comments on Stalin, though banal in the extreme, are nevertheless of interest in indicating at the same time, a disdain (reminiscent of Trotsky) for a leader whose power was based entirely on bureaucratic manipulation, and a grudging respect for a formidable opponent.[18]

Stalin is one of the most extraordinary figures in world history. He began as a small clerk, and he has never stopped being a clerk. Stalin owes nothing to rhetoric. He governs from his office, thanks to a bureaucracy that obeys his every nod and gesture. . . .

Stalin pretends to have been the herald of the Bolshevik revolution. In actual fact, he identifies himself with the Russia of the Tsars, and he has merely resurrected the tradition of Pan-Slavism.

---

[17] From *The Ribbentrop Memoirs*, trans. Oliver Watson (London: Weidenfeld and Nicolson, Ltd., 1954), p. 113. Originally in *Zwischen London und Moskau, Erinnerungen und letzte Aufzeichnungen. Aus dem Nachlass herausgegeben von Annelies von Ribbentrop* (Leoni am Starnberger See, 1953), pp. 182 f. Copyright 1953 by Druffel-Verlag. Reprinted by permission of the publishers.

[18] From *Hitler's Secret Conversations 1941-1944*, pp. 8, 182, 624. Copyright 1953 by Farrar, Straus and Young, Inc. Reprinted by permission of Farrar, Straus and Giroux, Inc., New York, and Weidenfeld and Nicolson, Ltd., London.

For him Bolshevism is only a means, a disguise designed to trick the Germanic and Latin peoples. . . .

Stalin is half beast, half giant. To the social side of life he is utterly indifferent. The people can rot, for all he cares. . . .

CHURCHILL: "DEEPLY IMPRESSED"

Sir Winston Churchill's accounts of his wartime dealings with Stalin afford many revealing insights into the Soviet dictator's character and political methods. The extracts reproduced here relate to the first meeting of the two leaders in August 1942. Churchill's purpose in visiting Moscow was to break the bad news to Stalin that there would be no Second Front in France in 1942, and to inform him of alternative Anglo-American plans.[19]

The first two hours were bleak and sombre. I began at once with the question of the Second Front, saying that I wished to speak frankly and would like to invite complete frankness from Stalin. . . . Stalin, whose glumness had by now much increased, said that as he understood it, we were unable to create a second front with any large force and unwilling even to land six divisions. I said that this was so. We could land six divisions, but the landing of them would be more harmful than helpful, for it would greatly injure the big operation planned for next year. War was war but not folly, and it would be folly to invite a disaster which would help nobody. . . . Stalin, who had become restless, said that his view about war was different. A man who was not prepared to take risks could not win a war. Why were we so afraid of the Germans? He could not understand. His experience showed that troops must be blooded in battle. . . . I inquired whether he had ever asked himself why Hitler did not come to England in 1940. . . . The fact was that Hitler was afraid of the operation. It is not so easy to cross the Channel. Stalin replied that this was no analogy. . . . [After further exchanges this part of the conversation ended in "an oppressive silence." Churchill succeeded in re-

[19] From Winston S. Churchill, *The Second World War*, Vol. IV: *The Hinge of Fate* (London: Cassell and Company, Ltd.; Boston: Houghton Mifflin Company), pp. 430, 431, 433, 434. Reprinted by permission of the publishers. Extracts are taken from the Cassell edition.

lieving the tension somewhat by talking of the bombing of Germany—ED.]

The moment had now come to bring "Torch" into action. . . . As I told the whole story Stalin became intensely interested. His first question was what would happen in Spain and Vichy France. A little later on he remarked that the operation was militarily right, but he had political doubts about the effect on France. . . . I then described the military advantages of freeing the Mediterranean, whence still another front could be opened. . . . To illustrate my point I had meanwhile drawn a picture of a crocodile, and explained to Stalin with the help of this picture how it was our intention to attack the soft belly of the crocodile as we attacked his hard snout. And Stalin, whose interest was now at a high pitch, said, "May God prosper this undertaking."

I emphasised that we wanted to take the strain off the Russians. . . . If North Africa were won this year we could make a deadly attack upon Hitler next year. This marked the turning point in our conversation. [Stalin then began to express doubts about certain political aspects, which Churchill and the United States representative Mr. Averell Harriman sought to allay—ED.] At this point Stalin seemed suddenly to grasp the strategic advantages of "Torch." He recounted four main reasons for it: first, it would hit Rommel in the back; second, it would overawe Spain; third, it would produce fighting between Germans and Frenchmen in France; and fourth, it would expose Italy to the whole brunt of the war.

I was deeply impressed with this remarkable statement. It showed the Russian Dictator's swift and complete mastery of a problem hitherto novel to him. Very few people alive could have comprehended in so few minutes the reasons which we had all so long been wrestling with for months. He saw it all in a flash.

DEANE: "COURAGEOUS BUT CAUTIOUS"

Major General John R. Deane, who had the opportunity of observing Stalin while negotiating with Soviet officials on United States military assistance during World War II, gives here an American military man's appreciation of Stalin's character, manner, and political talents.[20]

[20] John R. Deane, "Negotiating on Military Assistance, 1943-1945," from *Negotiating with the Russians*, ed. Raymond Dennett and Joseph E. Johnson (Boston: World Peace Foundation, 1951), pp. 21-22. Copyright 1951 by World Peace Foundation. Reprinted by permission of World Peace Foundation.

To start with, Stalin is the leader of an unlimited autocracy with power as absolute as that of Ivan the Terrible or Peter the Great. Seeing him in company with individuals of the Politburo, such as Molotov or Mikoyan, one is convinced that the power of decision is his alone. He listens to his advisors, but appears to feel no constraint in brushing aside whatever point of view they may be pressing. . . .

In appearance, Stalin is unprepossessing. He is short and color-less. It may be that it is his lack of color or desire for it that is his greatest strength. He seems to be completely indifferent as to what others might think of him and pays little or no attention to any of the social graces. One gets the impression that a physical tough-ening of early days is giving way to a pallid paunchiness developed by the more sedentary habits of later years. He shows the marks of his 71 years [Stalin was 71 in 1950—Ed.] in the deep wrinkles of his skin and the gray thinness of what once must have been thick black hair. He betrays little emotion and his manner is neither pleasant nor unpleasant. It is markedly indifferent. I have seen him smile, but I have not heard him laugh. I have never seen him unduly agitated. He has all the attributes of a good poker player.

As to his character, I would say Stalin is courageous, but cautious. He can act quickly and decisively or wait with infinite patience. He can be kind or merciless as the spirit moves him. He has a keen intellect and more than ordinary intelligence. He knows political values—the people are seldom out of sight of his statue or his picture, which is plastered over all of the Soviet Union most of the time. He fawns over children in public. He can slap backs with the same ease that he can slit throats. His blind spots result from the narrow confines of ideological fanaticism in which his life has run.

WALTER BEDELL SMITH:
A POST WORLD WAR II IMPRESSION

After 1946 the onset of the Cold War led to a sharp nar-rowing of opportunities for Westerners to observe or speak with Stalin. Walter Bedell Smith, United States Ambassador to Moscow, 1946-49, records here his own impressions of the aging dictator during this period.[21]

[21] From Walter Bedell Smith, *My Three Years in Moscow* (New York: J. B. Lippincott Company; London: William Heinemann Ltd., 1949), pp. 47-48. Copyright 1949 by Walter Bedell Smith and reprinted by permission of the publishers.

Met face to face, Stalin is not by any means the unattractive personality which some writers have depicted. Indeed, he has genuine charm when he chooses to exercise it. While not tall, he is square and erect, giving the impression of great strength. Since the beginning of the war, he has abandoned his old party uniform of khaki trousers and a plain tunic that buttoned up to the neck, on which he wore no insignia, and he now appears in public and receives foreign visitors in the uniform of a Marshal of the Soviet Union, with usually only a single decoration—the treasured gold star of a Hero of the Soviet Union.

I scarcely noticed the pockmarks which some American writers have emphasized. The most attractive feature of Stalin's face is his fine dark eyes, which light up when he is interested. They did not impress me either as "gentle," as one observer thought, or "cold as steel," as others have remarked, but they are alert, expressive and intelligent. His manner is calm, slow and self-assured, and when he wishes to warm up during a conversation he seems at times actually benign. There is no question but that he can be brutally abrupt, and I have been told that he has sometimes referred to himself, half-apologetically, as "a rude old man."

DJILAS: CONVERSATIONS WITH STALIN

Milovan Djilas, the Montenegrin communist writer, was for many years one of Tito's three closest collaborators, but was expelled from the Yugoslav leadership in 1954 and subsequently imprisoned for his writings which brilliantly analyzed the bureaucratization of communist society (notably The New Class). *On three occassions, in 1944, 1945, and 1948, Djilas visited Moscow for talks with Stalin, and these visits are recorded in his book* Conversations with Stalin. *Written as it is by a leading foreign communist who had the opportunity to observe at close quarters the inner circle of the Soviet leadership and who was at the same time a first-class writer and a reporter of impeccable integrity, this work presents a picture of the aging Stalin unparalleled in its fullness and immediacy. Our extracts begin with Djilas's first encounter with Stalin in March 1944.*[22]

■ From Milovan Djilas *Conversations with Stalin*, pp. 60-62, 69-70, 75-77, 105, 110-11, 114-15, 152-54. Copyright © 1962 by Harcourt, Brace and World, Inc., and reprinted with their permission.

Stalin was in a marshal's uniform and soft boots, without any medals except a golden star—the Order of Hero of the Soviet Union, on the left side of his breast. In his stance there was nothing artificial or posturing. This was not that majestic Stalin of the photographs or the newsreels—with the stiff, deliberate gait and posture. He was not quiet for a moment. He toyed with his pipe, which bore the white dot of the English firm Dunhill, or drew circles with a blue pencil around words indicating the main subjects for discussion, which he then crossed out with slanting lines as each part of the discussion was nearing an end, and he kept turning his head this way and that while he fidgeted in his seat.

I was also surprised at something else: he was of very small stature and ungainly build. His torso was short and narrow, while his legs and arms were too long. His left arm and shoulder seemed rather stiff. He had a quite large paunch, and his hair was sparse, though his scalp was not completely bald. His face was white, with ruddy cheeks. Later I learned that this coloration, so characteristic of those who sit long in offices, was known as the "Kremlin complexion" in high Soviet circles. His teeth were black and irregular, turned inward. Not even his mustache was thick or firm. Still the head was not a bad one; it had something of the folk, the peasantry, the paterfamilias about it—with those yellow eyes and a mixture of sternness and roguishness.

I was also surprised at his accent. One could tell that he was not a Russian. Nevertheless his Russian vocabulary was rich, and his manner of expression very vivid and plastic, and replete with Russian proverbs and sayings. As I later became convinced, Stalin was well acquainted with Russian literature—though only Russian —but the only real knowledge he had outside of Russian limits was his knowledge of political history.

One thing did not surprise me: Stalin had a sense of humor—a rough humor, self-assured, but not entirely without finesse and depth. His reactions were quick and acute—and conclusive, which did not mean that he did not hear the speaker out, but it was evident that he was no friend of long explanations. Also remarkable was his relation to Molotov. He obviously regarded the latter as a very close associate, as I later confirmed.[23] Molotov was the only member of the Politburo whom Stalin addressed with the familiar pronoun *ty*, which is in itself significant when it is kept in mind

[23] Compare Hilger's observations on Stalin's special relationship to Molotov— "Hilger: The Compleat Decision-Maker," above.

that with Russians the polite form *vy* is normal even among very close friends. . . .

We no sooner entered a small hall from the entrance than Stalin appeared—this time in shoes and dressed in his plain tunic, buttoned up to his chin, and known so well from his prewar pictures. Like this he seemed even smaller, but also simpler and completely at home. He led us into a small and surprisingly empty study—no books, no pictures, just bare wooden walls. We seated ourselves around a small writing table, and he immediately began to inquire about events concerning the Yugoslav Supreme staff.

The very manner of his inquiry showed a sharp contrast between Stalin and Molotov. With Molotov not only his thoughts but also the process of their generation was impenetrable. Similarly his mentality remained sealed and incrutable. Stalin, however, was of a lively, almost restless temperament. He always questioned—himself and others; and he argued—with himself and others. . . . Stalin was no less a cold calculator than he. But precisely because his was a more passionate and many-sided nature—though all sides were equal and so convincing that it seemed he never dissembled but was always truly experiencing each of his roles—he was more penetrable and offered greater possibilities. . . . For Stalin, too, everything was transitory. But that was his philosophical view. Behind that impermanence and within it, certain great and final ideals lay hidden—his ideals, which he could approach by manipulating or kneading the reality and the living men who comprised it. . . .[24]

In his memoirs Churchill vividly describes an improvised dinner with Stalin at the Kremlin.[25] But this is the way Stalin's dinners were in general.

In a spacious and unadorned, though tasteful, dining room, the front half of a long table was covered with all kinds of foods on warmed heavy silver platters as well as beverages and plates and other utensils. Everyone served himself and sat where he wished around the free half of the table. Stalin never sat at the head, but he always sat in the same chair—the first to the left of the head of the table.

The variety of food and drink was enormous—with meats and hard liquor predominating. But everything else was simple and

[24] This penetrating remark may be compared with Tucker's analysis of Stalin's "transformism," chapter 3.

[25] See Winston S. Churchill, *The Second World War,* Vol. IV: *The Hinge of Fate,* pp. 445-47.

unostentatious. None of the servants appeared except when Stalin rang, and the only occasion for this was when I requested beer. Everyone ate what he pleased and as much as he wanted; only there was rather too much of urging and daring us to drink and there were too many toasts.

Such a dinner usually lasted six or more hours—from ten at night till four or five in the morning. One ate and drank slowly, during a rambling conversation which ranged from stories and anecdotes to the most serious political and even philosophical subjects. Unofficially and in actual fact a significant part of Soviet policy was shaped at these dinners. Besides they were the most frequent and most convenient entertainment and only luxury in Stalin's otherwise monotonous and somber life. . . .

At these dinners the Soviet leaders were at their closest, most intimate with one another. Everyone would tell the news from his bailiwick, whom he had met that day, and what plans he was making. The sumptuous table and considerable, though not immoderate, quantities of alcohol enlivened spirits and intensified the atmosphere of cordiality and informality. An uninstructed visitor might hardly have detected any difference between Stalin and the rest. Yet it existed. His opinion was carefully noted. No one opposed him very hard. It all rather resembled a patriarchal family with a crotchety head whose foibles always caused the home folks to be apprehensive.

Stalin took quantities of food that would have been enormous even for a much larger man. He usually picked meat, which reflected his mountaineer origins. He also liked all kinds of specialties, in which this land of various climes and civilizations abounded, but I did not notice that any one food was his particular favorite. He drank moderately, most frequently mixing red wine and vodka in little glasses. I never noticed any signs of drunkenness in him. . . .

[Later Djilas ran afoul of the Soviet leadership for his critical remarks on the misconduct of Soviet troops occupying northeastern Yugoslavia. His visit to Moscow in April 1945 occurred when this incident was still rankling—ED.]

Thereupon Stalin asked me about the affair of the Red Army. I explained to him that it had not been my intention to insult the Red Army, but that I had wished to call attention to irregularities of certain of its members and to the political difficulties they were creating for us.

Stalin interrupted: "Yes, you have, of course, read Dostoevsky?

Do you see what a complicated thing is man's soul, man's psyche? Well then, imagine a man who has fought from Stalingrad to Belgrade—over thousands of kilometers of his own devastated land, across the dead bodies of his comrades and dearest ones! How can such a man react normally? And what is so awful in his having fun with a woman, after such horrors? You have imagined the Red Army to be ideal. And it is not ideal, nor can it be, even if it did not contain a certain percentage of criminals—we opened up our penitentiaries and stuck everybody into the army. There was an interesting case. An Air Force major had fun with a woman, and a chivalrous engineer appeared to protect her. The Major drew a gun: 'Ekh, you mole from the rear!'—and he killed the chivalrous engineer. They sentenced the Major to death. But somehow the matter was brought before me, and I made inquiries—I have the right as commander in chief in time of war—and I released the Major and sent him to the front. Now he is one of our heroes. One has to understand the soldier. The Red Army is not ideal. The important thing is that it fights Germans—and it is fighting them well, while the rest doesn't matter."

Soon after, upon my return from Moscow, I heard, to my horror, of a far more significant example of Stalin's "understanding" attitude toward the sins of Red Army personnel. Namely, while crossing East Prussia, Soviet soldiers, especially the tank units, pounded and regularly killed all German civilian refugees—women and children. Stalin was informed of this and asked what should be done. He replied: "We lecture our soldiers too much; let them have some initiative!" . . .

Stalin presented his views on the distinctive nature of the war that was being waged: "This war is not as in the past; whoever occupies a territory also imposes on it his own social system. Everyone imposes his own system as far as his army can reach. It cannot be otherwise."

He also pointed out, without going into long explanations, the meaning of his Panslavic policy. "If the Slavs keep united and maintain solidarity, no one in the future will be able to move a finger. Not even a finger!" he repeated, emphasizing his thought by cleaving the air with his forefinger.

Someone expressed doubt that the Germans would be able to recuperate within fifty years. But Stalin was of a different opinion. "No, they will recover, and very quickly. That is a highly developed industrial country with an extremely qualified and numerous working class and technical intelligentsia. Give them twelve to fifteen

years and they'll be on their feet again. And this is why the unity
of the Slavs is important. But even apart from this, if the unity of
the Slavs exists, no one will dare move a finger."

At one point he got up, hitched up his pants as though he was
about to wrestle or to box, and cried out almost in a transport,
"The war shall soon be over. We shall recover in fifteen or twenty
years, and then we'll have another go at it."

There was something terrible in his words: a horrible war was
still going on. Yet there was something impressive, too, about his
cognizance of the paths he had to take, the inevitability that faced
the world in which he lived and the movement that he headed.' . . .

[The following revealing incident involving Kalinin, the President of the Supreme Soviet Presidium, occurred at a banquet given
in honor of the Yugoslav leaders—ED.]

Certainly Stalin knew of Kalinin's decreptitude, for he made
heavy-footed fun of him when the latter asked Tito for a Yugoslav cigarette. "Don't take any—those are capitalist cigarettes," said
Stalin, and Kalinin confusedly dropped the cigarette from his
trembling fingers, whereupon Stalin laughed and his physiognomy
took on the expression of a satyr. . . .

[Finally Djilas shows us Stalin as he saw him in 1948, shortly
before the Soviet-Yugoslav break. This was the Stalin who was to
rule Russia for five more years. The conversation about the Jews
gives a rare glimpse of Stalin's anti-Semitism, which became increasingly apparent in his postwar policies, culminating in the
"doctors' plot" allegations on the eve of his death—ED.]

It was incomprehensible how much he had changed in two or
three years. When I had last seen him, in 1945, he was still lively,
quick-witted, and had a pointed sense of humor. But that was
during the war, and it had been, it would seem, Stalin's last effort
and limit. Now he laughed at inanities and shallow jokes. On
one occasion he not only failed to get the political point of an
anecdote I told him in which he outsmarted Churchill and Roosevelt, but I had the impression that he was offended, in the manner
of old men. I perceived an awkward astonishment on the faces of
the rest of the party.

In one thing, though, he was still the Stalin of old: stubborn,
sharp, suspicious whenever anyone disagreed with him. He even
cut Molotov, and one could feel the tension between them. Everyone paid court to him, avoiding any expression of opinion before
he expressed his, and then hastening to agree with him.

Toward the end of the dinner Stalin unexpectedly asked me

why there were not many Jews in the Yugoslav Party and why these few played no important role in it. I tried to explain to him that there were not many Jews in Yugoslavia to begin with, and most belonged to the middle class. I added, "The only prominent Communist Jew is Pijade, and he regards himself as being more of a Serb than a Jew."

Stalin began to recall: "Pijade, short, with glasses? Yes, I remember, he visited me. And what is his position?"

"He is a member of the Central Committee, a veteran Communist, the translator of *Das Kapital*," I explained.

"In our Central Committee there are no Jews!" he broke in, and began to laugh tauntingly. "You are an anti-Semite, you, too, Djilas, you, too, are an anti-Semite!"

I took his words and laughter to mean the opposite, as I should have—as the expression of his own anti-Semitism and as a provocation to get me to declare my stand concerning the Jews, particularly Jews in the Communist movement.

5
Points of View

It is doubtful if any historical figure has evoked in his own lifetime more numerous and contradictory attempts at evaluating his achievements and historical significance than Stalin. The present chapter brings together excerpts from the most influential of such evaluations (by Trotsky, Souvarine, and Deutscher) and from others illustrative of the more important partisan viewpoints (by Barbusse, Lyons, and Murphy). The popular biographies, however, were rarely purely commercial in motivation, but usually political as well. The best of them are interesting sources not so much on Stalin as on the intellectual history of the second quarter of the twentieth century, reflecting in turn the attitudes of the Popular Front period, the hostility of the aftermath of the great purges and during the Nazi-Soviet pact, the warm and uncritical appreciation during the period of the wartime alliance, or the disillusionment and Orwellian pessimism typical of the Cold War era. The chapter ends with a remarkably succinct summary and evaluation of Stalin's career by a contemporary Western statesman, Sir Anthony Eden. Limited in various ways and degrees by lack of knowledge, by the distortion of proximity, and by partisan commitment, such contemporary evaluations are nevertheless important, for the historical meaning of a great man cannot be understood without reference to what he meant to the men of his time.

BARBUSSE 1935: "THE LENIN OF TODAY" [1]

One may also say that it is in Stalin more than anyone else that the thoughts and words of Lenin are to be found. He is the Lenin of to-day.

[1] From Henri Barbusse, "Stalin: A New World Seen Through One Man" in *Stalin: A Biography* (London: John Lane, 1935), pp. 290-91. Reprinted by permission of Willis Kingsley King.

In many ways, as we have seen, he is extraordinarily like Vladimir Ilitch: he has the same knowledge of theory, the same practical common sense, the same firmness. In what way do they differ? Here are two opinions of Soviet workers: "Lenin was the leader: Stalin is the master." And also: "Lenin is a greater man, Stalin is a stronger. . . ." We will not, however, pursue these parallels too much as they might lead us to form a wrong idea of these two exceptionally great men, one of whom formed the other.

Let us say, if you like, that Lenin, especially because of circumstances, was more of an agitator. In the vast directing system which is now much better organized and more developed, Stalin must necessarily act far more through the medium of the Party, by the intermediary of organization, as it were. Stalin is not, nowadays, the man of great tempestuous meetings. However, he has never made use of that tumultuous force of eloquence which is the great asset of upstart tyrants and the only one, very often, of successful apostles: this is a point which should be considered carefully by historians who attempt to gauge him. It is by other paths that he came into and remains in contact with the working, peasant, and intellectual population of the U.S.S.R., and with the Revolutionaries of the world, who carry their spiritual country in their hearts —namely, many more than two hundred million people.

We have caught a glimpse of some of the secrets of his greatness. Among all the sources of his genius, which is the principal one? Bela Kun said, in a fine phrase: "He knows how not to go too quickly. *He knows how to weigh the moment.*" And Bela Kun considers that to be the chief characteristic of Stalin, the one which belongs to him in particular, much more than any other; to wait, to temporize, to resist alluring temptations and to be possessed of terrible patience. Is it not this power that has made Stalin, of all the Revolutionaries of history, the man who has most practically enriched the spirit of Revolution, and who has committed the fewest faults? He weighs the pros and cons and reflects a great deal before proposing anything (a great deal does not mean a long time). He is extremely circumspect and does not easily give his confidence. He said to one of his close associates, who distrusted a third party: "A reasonable amount of distrust is a good basis for collective work." He is as prudent as a lion.

SOUVARINE 1935: "THIS REPULSIVE CHARACTER" [2]

From the course of events, the tracing of history and the un-ravelling of texts, there emerges in sufficiently clear relief this repulsive character whose prodigious destiny it is so difficult to explain outside of the Soviet Union. We know now the abilities and the weaknesses of Stalin, the excessive disproportion between his intellect and his will, between his knowledge and his *savoir-faire,* and the reasons for his personal success gained over the ruins of the socialist programme of his Party. We have seen him patient, meticulous, wary of illusions as of words, and strong above all in his contempt for the individual and in his lack of principles and scruples. He is a product of circumstances, he owes his political fortune to his antagonists, though one can say as much of all his dictator contemporaries. He has not succeeded in establishing him-self without a certain flair, without natural faculties for intrigue and an effective alloy of coolness and energy. Clever at putting off disadvantageous solutions, at dividing his enemies and getting round obstacles, he shrinks before nothing if he can but attack, strike and crush. He had the dexterity to avoid in the Party the shedding of blood spilt so often in the country, to exhaust op-position by dilatory tactics combined with the gag, the pillory and the whole gamut of sanctions. We recognise him as cunning, crafty, treacherous, but also brutal, violent, implacable, and set always on the exclusive aim of holding the power he has confiscated by an accumulation of petty means. . . .

Stalin has obviously not read Machiavelli, still less the astound-ing *Dialogue in Hell between Machiavelli and Montesquieu,* an anonymous book published in exile by a proscribed republican of the Second Empire, Maurice Joly. But he has followed by instinct the line of conduct traced in this ironical manual of cheating and duplicity whose precepts can be summed up in these almost literal lines:

> Separate morality from politics, substitute force and astuteness for law, paralyse the individual intelligence, mislead the people with appearances, consent to liberty only under the weight of terror, pan-

[2] From Boris Souvarine, *Stalin: A Critical Survey of Bolshevism,* trans. C. L. R. James (New York: Alliance Book Corporation; London: Martin Secker & War-burg, Ltd., 1939), pp. 581-83. Reprinted by permission of Martin Secker & War-burg, Ltd. and The Ziff-Davis Publishing Company.

der to national prejudices, keep concealed from the country what is happening in the world and likewise from the capital what is happening in the provinces, transform the instruments of thought into instruments of power, remorselessly inflict executions without trials and administrative deportations, exact a perpetual apology for every act, teach the history of your reign yourself, employ the police as the keystone of the regime, create faithful followers by means of ribbons and baubles, build up the cult of the usurper into a kind of religion, create a void around you thus making yourself indispensable, weaken public opinion until it subsides in apathy, impress your name everywhere as drops of water hollow out granite, profit by the ease with which men turn informers, manipulate society by means of its vices, speak as little as possible, say the opposite of what you think, and change the very meaning of words. . . .

All this appears to have been written for Stalin, and resolves the oft-discussed problem of the traits common to Lenin and his heir.

TROTSKY 1940: "THE MACHINE BOSS" [3]

Stalin represents a phenomenon utterly exceptional. He is neither a thinker, a writer nor an orator. He took possession of power before the masses had learned to distinguish his figure from others during the triumphal processions across Red Square. Stalin took possession of power, not with the aid of personal qualities, but with the aid of an impersonal machine. And it was not he who created the machine, but the machine that created him. That machine, with its force and its authority, was the product of the prolonged and heroic struggle of the Bolshevik Party, which itself grew out of ideas. The machine was the bearer of the idea before it became an end in itself. Stalin headed the machine from the moment he cut off the umbilical cord that bound it to the idea and it became a thing unto itself. Lenin created the machine through constant association with the masses, if not by oral word, then by printed word, if not directly, then through the medium of his disciples. Stalin did not create the machine but took possession of it.

[3] From Leon Trotski, *Stalin: An Appraisal of the Man and His Influence*, ed. and trans. Charles Malamuth (London: Hollis and Carter, 1947), pp. xv, 336-37, 384-87, 392. Reprinted by permission of the Bodley Head, Ltd. Trotsky was putting the final touches to his biography of Stalin when he was assassinated in 1940. The sections in square brackets are reconstructions by the editor-translator of Trotsky's text, parts of which were spattered with blood or otherwise damaged in Trotsky's struggle with his assassin.

For this, exceptional and special qualities were necessary. But they were not the qualities of the historic initiator, thinker, writer, or orator. The machine had grown out of ideas. Stalin's first qualification was a contemptuous attitude toward ideas. . . .

It is impossible to understand Stalin and his latter-day success without understanding the mainspring of his personality: love of power, ambition, envy—active, never-slumbering envy of all who are more gifted, more powerful, rank higher than he. With that characteristic braggadocio which is the essence of Mussolini, he told one of his friends: "I have never met my equal." Stalin could never have uttered this phrase, even to his most intimate friends, because it would have sounded too crude, too absurd, too ridiculous. There were any number of men on the Bolshevik staff alone who excelled Stalin in all respects but one—his concentrated ambition. Lenin highly valued power as a tool of action. But pure love of power was utterly alien to him. Not so with Stalin. Psychologically, power to him was always something apart from the purposes which it was supposed to serve. The desire to exert his will as the athlete exerts his muscles, to lord it over others—that was the mainspring of his personality. His will thus acquired an ever-increasing concentration of force, swelling in aggressiveness, activity, range of expression, stopping at nothing. The more often Stalin had occasion to convince himself that he was lacking in very many attributes for the acquisition of power, the more intensely did he compensate for each deficiency of character, the more subtly did he transform each lack into an advantage under certain conditions.

The current official comparisons of Stalin to Lenin are simply indecent. If the basis of comparison is sweep of personality, it is impossible to place Stalin even alongside Mussolini or Hitler. However meager the "ideas" of Fascism, both of the victorious leaders of reaction, the Italian and the German, from the very beginning of their respective movements displayed initiative, roused the masses to action, pioneered new paths through the political jungle. Nothing of the kind can be said about Stalin. The Bolshevik Party was created by Lenin. Stalin grew out of its political machine and remained inseparable from it. He has never had any other approach to the masses or to the events of history than through this machine. In the first period of his rise to power he was himself caught unawares by his own success. He took his steps without certainty, looking to right and left and over his shoulder, always ready to slink back or run to cover. Used as a counterweight against me, he was bolstered and encouraged by Zinoviev and Kamenev, and to a lesser extent by Rykov, Bukharin and Tomsky. No one thought at the time that Stalin would some day loom away above their heads. . . .

A political reaction set in after the prodigious strain of the Revolution and the Civil War. . . . In 1923 the situation began to stabilize. The Civil War, like the War with Poland, was definitely in the past. The most horrible consequences of the famine had been overcome, the NEP had given impetus to a vitalizing revival of national economy. The constant shifting of Communists from post to post, from one sphere of activity to another soon became the exception rather than the rule. Communists began to acquire permanent positions, [berths that were their own and led to higher positions, and they] began to rule in a planned fashion the regions or districts of economic and political life entrusted to their administrative discretion. [They were rapidly turning into officials, into bureaucrats, as] the placement of Party members and officials acquired a more systematic and planned character. No longer were assignments to duty regarded as temporary and almost fortuitous. The question of appointments came to have more and more to do with the question of personal life, living conditions of the [appointee's] family, his career.

It was then that Stalin began to emerge with increasing prominence as the organizer, the assigner of tasks, the dispenser of jobs, the trainer and master of the bureaucracy. He chose his men by their hostility or indifference toward his various opponents and particularly toward him whom he regarded as his chief opponent, the chief obstacle in the path of his progress upward. Stalin generalized and classified his own administrative experience, chiefly the experience of systematic conniving behind the scenes, and made it available to those most closely associated with him. He taught them to organize their local political machines on the pattern of his own machine: how to recruit collaborators, how to utilize their weaknesses, how to set comrades at odds with each other, how to run the machine.

As the life of the bureaucracy grew in stability, it generated an increasing need of comfort. Stalin rode in on the crest of this spontaneous movement for creature comfort, guiding it, harnessing it to his own designs. He rewarded the most loyal with the most attractive and advantageous positions. He set the limits on the benefits to be derived from these positions. He hand-picked the membership of the Control Commission, instilling in many of them the need of ruthlessly persecuting the deviators. At the same time he instructed them to look through their fingers at the exceptionally extravagant mode of life led by the officials loyal to the General Secretary. For Stalin measured every situation, every political circumstance, every combination of people [by one criterion—usefulness] to himself, to his struggle for power, to his relentless itch for domination over others.

Everything else was intellectually beyond his depth. He was pushing two of his strongest competitors into a fight. He raised his talent for utilizing personal and group antagonisms to a fine art, an inimitable art in the sense that he had developed an almost faultless instinct for it. In each new situation his first and foremost consideration was how he personally could benefit. Whenever the interests of the whole came into conflict with his personal interests, he always without exception sacrificed the interests of the whole. On all occasions, under any pretext and whatever the result, he did everything possible to make difficulties for his stronger competitors. With the same persistence he tried to reward every act of personal loyalty. Secretly at first and then more openly, equality was proclaimed a petty-bourgeois prejudice. He came out in defense of inequality, in defense of special privileges for the higherups of the bureaucracy.

In this deliberate demoralization Stalin was never interested in distant perspectives. Nor did he think through to the social significance of this process in which he was playing the leading role. He acted . . . like the empiricist he is. He selects those loyal to him and rewards them; he helps them to secure privileged positions; he requires of them the repudiation of personal political purposes. He teaches them how to create for themselves the necessary machinery for influencing the masses and for holding the masses in submission. Never does he consider that his policy runs directly counter to the struggle that engaged Lenin's interest more and more during the last year of his life—the struggle against bureaucracy. He himself speaks occasionally of bureaucracy, but always in the most abstract and lifeless terms. He has in mind lack of attention, red tape, the untidiness of offices and the like, but he is deaf and blind to the formation of a whole privileged caste welded together by the bond of honor among thieves, by their common interest [as privileged exploiters of the whole body politic] and by their ever-growing remoteness from the people. Without suspecting it, Stalin is organizing not only a new political machine but a new caste.

He approaches matters only from the point of view of selecting cadres, improving the machine, securing his personal control over it, his personal power. No doubt it seems to him, in so far as he is at all concerned with general questions, that his machine will invest the government with greater strength and stability, and thus assure the further development of socialism in a separate country. Beyond that he does not venture to generalize. That the crystallization of a new ruling stratum of professional officials, placed in a privileged situation and camouflaged from the masses by the idea of socialism—that the formation of this new arch-privileged and arch-powerful ruling stratum changes the social structure of the state and to a considerable and ever-growing extent the social composition of the new society—is a consideration that he refuses to contemplate; and whenever it is suggested, he waves it away with his arms or with his revolver. Thus, Stalin, the empiricist, without formally breaking with the revolutionary tradition, without repudiating Bolshevism, became [the most effective betrayer and destroyer of both.] . . .

In the spring of 1924, after one of the Plenums of the Central Committee at which I was not present because of illness, I said to [I. N.] Smirnov: "Stalin will become the dictator of the U.S.S.R." Smirnov knew Stalin well. They had shared revolutionary work and exile together for years, and under such conditions people get to know each other best of all.

"Stalin?" he asked me with amazement. "But he is a mediocrity, a colorless nonentity."

"Mediocrity, yes; nonentity, no," I answered him. "The dialectics of history have already hooked him and will raise him up. He is needed by all of them—by the tired radicals, by the bureaucrats, by the *nepmen,* the *kulaks,* the upstarts, the sneaks, by all the worms that are crawling out of the upturned soil of the manured revolution. He knows how to meet them on their own ground, he speaks their language and he knows how to lead them. He has the deserved reputation of an old revolutionist, which makes him invaluable to them as a blinder on the eyes of the country. He has will and daring. He will not hesitate to utilize them and to move them against the Party. He has already started doing this. Right now he is organizing around himself the sneaks of the Party, the artful dodgers. Of course, great developments in Europe, in Asia and in our country may intervene and upset all the speculations. But if everything continues to go automatically as it is going now, then Stalin will just as automatically become dictator."

In 1926 I had an argument with Kamenev, who insisted that Stalin was "just a small town politician." There was of course a particle of truth in that sarcastic characterization, but only a particle. Such attributes of character as slyness, faithlessness, the ability to exploit the lowest instincts of human nature are developed to an extraordinary degree in Stalin and, considering his strong character, represent mighty weapons in a struggle. Not, of course, any struggle. The struggle to liberate the masses requires other attributes. But in selecting men for privileged positions, in welding them together in the spirit of the caste, in weakening and disciplining the masses, Stalin's attributes were truly invaluable and rightfully make him the leader of the bureaucratic reaction. [Nevertheless,] Stalin remains a mediocrity. His mind is not only devoid of range but is even incapable of logical thinking. Every phrase of his speech has some immediate practical aim. But his speech as a whole never rises to a logical structure.

If Stalin could have foreseen at the very beginning where his fight against Trotskyism would lead, he undoubtedly would have stopped short, in spite of the prospect of victory over all his opponents. But he did not foresee anything. The prophecies of his opponents that he would become the leader of the Thermidor, the grave digger of the Party of the Revolution, seemed to him empty imaginings [and phrase-mongering]. He believed in the self-sufficiency of the Party machine, in its ability to perform all tasks. He did not have the slightest understanding of the historical function he was fulfilling. The absence of a creative imagination, the inability to generalize and to foresee killed the revolutionist in Stalin when he took the helm alone. But the very same traits backed by his authority as a former revolutionist enabled him to camouflage the rise of the Thermidorian bureaucracy.

LYONS 1940: "POWER FOR POWER'S SAKE" [4]

A significant difference between Stalin and his fellow-dictators, Hitler and Mussolini, is often overlooked. The *Duce* and the *Führer* possess the equipment of dynamic leadership. Both of them are spellbinders, rabble-rousers, supreme exhibitionists. They see

[4] From Eugene Lyons, *Stalin: Czar of All the Russians* (New York: J. B. Lippincott Company, 1940), pp. 286-90. Copyright 1940 by Eugene Lyons. Reprinted by permission of the publisher.

everything, are seen by everybody and manage to be everywhere at the same time. The abilities of the *Vozhd* are not merely more meager in these respects—they are of a totally different order.

Stalin is not an orator, as we have noted. I have heard his slow, labored, uninspired speech, in Russian strongly tinctured with his native Caucasian accent. He has neither the personal magnetism nor the epileptic zeal of his Teuton and Latin colleagues. He is essentially an *office dictator* who functions best in seclusion from his subjects, far-off and inaccessible in the grim shelter of his Kremlin hideout. Only once in his career as a dictator has he spoken on the radio. When he speaks at all, which is rarely, he chooses hand-picked audiences of specialists or party and government functionaries.

I have watched the other two dictators in action. They are shrill, pyrotechnic, full of hysterical gestures. Stalin, as I noted in my interview with him, speaks slowly, moves deliberately, with an almost complete absence of gesture. There is about the man something deeply Oriental—infinitely cautious, brooding, inward. On the surface he seems relaxed, but within he is tensed to spring. He gives a feeling of boundless energy and emotion held in leash by an iron will.

Stalin's cruelty is not angry and impulsive, like Hitler's or Mussolini's, but far more terrible: quiet, patient, carefully planned. And his policies, too, for the most part have the same character. Indeed, the merging of his destiny, for the time being, with Hitler's illustrates this. To the world it seemed sudden. Actually it was the product of long scheming, superhuman persistence on Stalin's part. In judging his every move on the larger world stage where he had injected himself so ponderously, this capacity for deliberate, long-term connivance must not be left out of the reckoning. Psychologically it gives him a certain advantage over the more theatrical and impetuous dictators with whom he deals.

The population of the Soviet capital is vouchsafed a flitting glimpse of their dictator at rare intervals, as it rolls in massed formation under clouds of banners across Red Square, cheering hoarsely. On these grand parade occasions Stalin looks down from the parapet of Lenin's granite tomb, bored and candidly contemptuous of the crowds. But there is also an edge of embarrassment in the wave of his hand in response to the cheers. He is not at home with crowds. That ability to flatter the rabble which is second nature to the other dictators is totally absent in Stalin. He knows that his authority does not depend on the masses, but on his tight grip on and shrewd manipulation of the political strings clutched in his fists. He did not climb to power on the shoulders of the mob, but through the labyrinthine corridors of inner party politics.

Stalin is a recluse and an introvert—a man living inside his own shell. He has no friends, but only underlings; no political allies, but only flatterers. All those who have been close to him and dared to speak afterwards have remarked on the symptoms of his profound feelings of inferiority. His ambitions and cruelties, his pathological craving for vengeance are aspects of these feelings. He is too intelligent not to savor the spuriousness of the adulation, not to despise the adulators. Yet he craves more and still more of the counterfeit salve. The sense of inadequateness that has obsessed him from childhood cannot be exorcised by success alone. He must have tangible proofs of greatness and dominion—in more obsequious praise, more executions, more conquests at home and abroad.

On the mental level his inferiorities are most sensitive. He is impelled to make friends with men of culture and patronize the arts. . . . But this excessive kindness to a few, a symbolic comradeship with genius, does not interfere with his harshness to intellectuals. . . . A list of those whom he has liquidated in these categories would sound like a roster of present-day Russian genius. . . .

Despite the natural curiosity that attaches to the dictator's private existence, it is really of no importance. Stalin belongs so completely to his career that the two cannot be separated. Caucasians are by reputation lusty lovers of wine, women and song. Stalin's larger obsessions have superseded these minor indulgences. It is as though his hunger for power had swallowed up all lesser appetites of the senses. He craves power not for what it can give in luxury and physical satisfaction but only as a basis for more power, like those nerve-sick misers who gather money for its own sake. He has not changed his own simple way of life as his power expanded. The knowledge that his slightest wish is law, that 180,000,000 people depend on his mood and tremble at his command are apparently the satisfactions on which his spirit thrives.

MURPHY: "STALIN THE GREAT" [5]

To-day, as we trace his course in retrospect, his aims and his path stand out clearly. Convinced that the proletariat must secure

[5] From J. T. Murphy, *Stalin: 1879-1944* (London: John Lane The Bodley Head, 1945), pp. 239, 242. Reprinted by permission of The Bodley Head and Curtis Brown, Ltd.

political power and become the leading class in society in order to transform it into the classless society of Socialism and Communism, he joined the party of Lenin dedicated to this task. Lenin's party purposed to make allies of other oppressed classes, especially the peasantry, and to conquer Czarism and the landlord, and capitalist classes.

By accomplishing these ends Lenin and Stalin led the way to government in the interests of the working people. . . .

The methods whereby Lenin, and later Stalin, accomplished these aims likewise stand out as unequivocally as the goal to which they aspired. They were governed by definite principles. Scientifically analysing the structure of society founded on private ownership of the means of production, they concluded that it is characterised by a condition of class warfare, is governed by the interests of the paramount economic classes, and must ever remain so until the means of production are socialised. Nevertheless, they rejected the theory that society develops everywhere under the same conditions and at the same tempo. They were convinced that while the class conflict was universal, it was also variable, and the working-class of each country or group of countries must conquer power separately in its own time and fashion and under its own leaders. They were also convinced that the conditions of the Russian Empire were such that the Russian working-class would be the first to succeed. Having conquered, the Russian workers would have to face the universal disapproval and hatred of the capitalist States and defend the Socialist State to the uttermost. . . .

"The World Revolution is not our creation. We only showed how to lead it and make a success of it in the interests of the great majority of humanity. We shall continue to do our duty."

Here we leave Joseph Stalin working in the Kremlin, the great human power-house of the changing world. No statesman of any country has emerged from this war with such gigantic achievements and such assured prospects to set before his people. When Nazism has been shattered there will be no European country in a position to challenge or endanger the U.S.S.R.; and in the Orient the destruction of Japanese imperialism will leave her eastern boundaries as unthreatened as her western. It will not be for Stalin to warn his people that great economic and political crises lie ahead in which everybody will have to work harder and be poorer. He can confidently face his people with frontiers secure and an era of economic and social expansion ahead such as the world has never known. The full power of the country's vast productive machinery and resources will be turned to healing the wounds of war and enriching the social well-being of every man, woman, and child in the Union.

Thus the new world, born on November 7th, 1917, will grow from strength to strength, and all men will testify that in its creation and development Joseph Stalin has earned his title of "the Great." But he himself will continue to prefer being known as a "disciple of Lenin."

DEUTSCHER: "THE FISTS AND FEET OF A GIANT" [6]

The impact of Lenin's illness on the Bolshevik leadership can hardly be exaggerated. The whole constellation ceased, almost at once, to shine with the reflected light of its master mind or to move in the familiar orbits. . . .

Stalin was in a sense less dependent on Lenin than were his colleagues; his intellectual needs were more limited than theirs. He was interested in the practical use of the Leninist gadgets, not in the Leninist laboratory of thought. His own behaviour was now dictated by the moods, needs, and pressures of the vast political machine that he had come to control. His political philosophy boiled down to securing the dominance of that machine by the handiest and most convenient means. . . .

The remarkable trait in Stalin was his unique sensibility to all those psychological undercurrents in and around the party, the untalked of hopes and tacit desires, of which he set himself up as a mouthpiece. . . .

In 1929, five years after Lenin's death, Soviet Russia embarked upon her second revolution, which was directed solely and exclusively by Stalin. In its scope and immediate impact upon the life of some 160 million people the second revolution was even more sweeping and radical than the first. It resulted in Russia's rapid industrialization; it compelled more than a hundred million peasants to abandon their small, primitive holdings and to set up collective farms; it ruthlessly tore the primeval wooden plough from the hands of the *muzhik* and forced him to grasp the wheel of a modern tractor; it drove tens of millions of illiterate people to school and made them learn to read and write; and spiritually it

[6] From I. Deutscher, *Stalin: A Political Biography* (London: Oxford University Press, 1949), pp. 235, 292, 294-95, 359-61, 364-65, 466-67. Reprinted by permission of the publisher.

detached European Russia from Europe and brought Asiatic Russia nearer to Europe. The rewards of that revolution were astounding; but so was its cost: the complete loss, by a whole generation, of spiritual and political freedom. . . .

And yet the giant's robe hangs somewhat loosely upon Stalin's figure. There is a baffling disproportion between the magnitude of the second revolution and the stature of its maker. . . . The ideas of the second revolution were not his. He neither foresaw it nor prepared for it. Yet he, and in a sense he alone, accomplished it. He was at first almost whipped into the vast undertaking by immediate dangers. He started it gropingly, and despite his own fears. Then, carried on by the force of his own doings, he walked the giant's causeway, almost without halt or rest. Behind him were tramping the myriads of weary and bleeding Russian feet, a whole generation in search of socialism in one country. His figure seemed to grow to mythical dimensions. Seen at close quarters, it was still the figure of a man of very ordinary stature and of middling thoughts. Only his fists and feet contrasted with his real stature—they were the fists and the feet of a giant. . . .

Describing the situation before and after the assassination of Kirov, we have referred to the traditional pattern of politics under Tsarist autocracy. This comparison may seem far-fetched, because of the gulf that separates Bolshevik from Tsarist Russia. Yet it was none other than Lenin who first hinted at the comparison. . . .

Lenin saw only the beginnings of the process by which defeated Tsarist Russia was imposing her own standards and methods upon victorious Bolshevism. The past took a cruel revenge upon a generation that was making a heroic effort to get away from it; and that revenge reached its climax precisely in the course of the second revolution. This paradox of Russian history became embodied in Stalin. More than anybody else he represented those 'responsible Communist administrators' whose 'culture' was still inferior to that of Russia's old rulers, and whose overwhelming inclination it was therefore to imitate, often unknowingly, the old rulers' customs and habits. . . . In this revenge of history, it was not so much the recent past as the remote one that seemed to chase and overtake the forward-moving nation. What was reasserting itself was the ferocious spirit of the early, pioneering, empire-building Tsars rather than the later, milder, more 'liberal' spirit of Tsardom in decay. The cruelty with which the past oppressed the present was proportionate to the determination with which the revolution had set out to repudiate the past.

Yet in Stalin the revolutionary elements, especially features inherited from Lenin, combined strangely with the traditional ones; and this combination made of him the most puzzling and elusive personality of his age. The past did not efface the revolution. It rather imprinted its own pattern on a new social substance. Like Cromwell as Lord Protector or Napoleon as Emperor, Stalin now remained the guardian and the trustee of the revolution. He consolidated its national gains and extended them. He 'built socialism'; and even his opponents, while denouncing his autocracy, admitted that most of his economic reforms were indeed essential for socialism. The revenge of the past thus bore not on his social programme but on his technique of government. It was mainly in that that the 'low and miserable' tradition of Tsardom came to predominate.

His technique of power, we know, revealed his distrustful attitude towards society, his pessimistic approach to it. Socialism was to be built by coercion rather than persuasion. Even where he attempted some sort of persuasion he more readily resorted to propagandist stunts than to enlightening argument. He drew, in other words, on that wide assortment of chicanery and trickery by which rulers of all ages and countries had held their peoples in subjection. As the revolution had proclaimed confidence in the people, that ·is in the working classes, to be its guiding principle, and as it had denounced political deception as serving class-oppression, the revenge of the past inevitably entailed a great conflict of ideas, a veritable spiritual crisis, which finally transformed the face of communism in this generation. This was the epilogue to the protracted conflict between authority, bent on moulding society exclusively from above, and society longing for freedom of self-determination. . . .

Not satisfied with dictating his will in all matters affecting the body politic, Stalin also aspired to be sole spiritual leader of his generation. He did so in part because his vanity had been hurt by the fact that the intellectual *élite* of Russia had hardly noticed him before he had brought them under his tutelage; and that even then they had at first treated his pronouncements on science, philosophy, and art with some irony. Apart from this, he had banished heresy from politics and economics only to find that the philosophical and literary journals bristled with heretical allusions. To venture out into these fields became for him a political necessity. Marxism had, in fact, shortened the distance between politics, philosophy, and literature. Stalin crudely over-simplified the Marxist view of their interconnexion, until he degraded science, history, and art to the point where they became handmaidens of his politics. Every time he issued a new economic and political directive, the historians, the philosophers, and the writers had to check carefully whether in their latest works they were not in conflict with the leader's last word. . . .

Many allied visitors who called at the Kremlin during the war were astonished to see on how many issues, great and small, military, political, or diplomatic, Stalin personally took the final decision. He was in effect his own commander-in-chief, his own minister of defence, his own quartermaster, his own minister of supply, his own foreign minister, and even his own *chef de protocole*. . . . Thus he went on, day after day, throughout four years of hostilities —a prodigy of patience, tenacity, and vigilance, almost omnipresent, almost omniscient.

EDEN: THE ACHIEVEMENT AND THE COST [7]

For a quarter of a century, Stalin ruled a vast empire in the manner of an eastern despot, made more terrible and more effective by a modern technique of persuasion and repression. Ruthlessly, he had driven his country into the front rank of the world's industrial powers. Against all expectation, he had mobilized the heroism of the Russian people, and urged them to the untold sacrifices which made possible the defeat of the German invader. The victory won, he gave no pause. His armies remained to hold in subjection the territories through which they had advanced to the west. He extracted from his exhausted countrymen their last ounce of strength to rebuild their devastated land, and to prepare for the next stage of communism's aggrandisement. However malign its purpose, the scale of Stalin's achievement was stupendous, dwarfed only by its cost in human suffering.

[7] From *The Memoirs of the R. Hon. Sir Anthony Eden K.G., P.C., M.C.: Full Circle* (London: Cassell and Company, Ltd.; New York: The Houghton Mifflin Company, 1960), p. 50. Copyright 1960 The Times Publishing Company, Ltd. Reprinted by permission of The Times Publishing Company, Ltd., Cassell and Company, Ltd., and The Houghton Mifflin Company.

6
The Cult of Personality and Its Consequences

It is not unusual for the subjects of a tyrant to attribute to him a plethora of exceptional human virtues or even superhuman powers. In part this appears to derive from the psychological needs of the tyrant himself, in part from the sycophancy of his court and in part from factors of mass psychology.

No doubt the Stalin cult is to be explained in some such terms as these. Many questions remain obscure, however. What weight should be attributed to each of the three sets of factors mentioned, in explaining its emergence? How far did the various stages in the development of the cult result from deliberate high-level decision, and how far was its evolution spontaneous? Do such contemporary phenomena as the Hitler cult in Germany and the Emperor cult in Japan provide instructive analogies, and if so what were the common factors making for their simultaneous emergence? Or is it more instructive to seek analogies in the despotisms of the ancient world or the orient? How far did different sections of the population, and at different times, "believe" what was said about Stalin? To what extent and in what ways was the cult exploited as a weapon in the struggles within Stalin's court?

We cannot pretend to answer these questions here, but it is essential to keep them in mind when considering the material on the cult reproduced below. This material illustrates the official view of Stalin from the 1930s on, which was valid not only in the U.S.S.R. itself, but throughout the international communist movement. But this official view of Stalin was also a political factor in its own right, a factor of enor-

mous importance in the whole pattern of totalitarian rule. In trying to understand this factor, we must obviously first know what it looked like. In addition, the image of Stalin projected in the cult obviously bore some relation to Stalin's own image of himself, although the relation has been little explored and remains obscure.

KIROV 1934: SEEDS OF THE CULT

Among the most energetic in building up the Stalin cult in its early stages was the Politburo member and Leningrad party leader Sergei Kirov. Ironically, Kirov's speech to the 1934 Leningrad conference, in which he made the oft-quoted remarks printed below, occurred a few short months before his assassination in circumstances which Soviet spokesmen now link closely with the triumph of "the cult of personality." [1]

It is not easy to grasp the figure of Stalin in all its gigantic proportions. In these latter years, ever since we have had to carry on our work without Lenin, there has been no major development in our labors, no innovation, slogan or trend of policy of any importance of which Comrade Stalin has not been the author. All the major work—and this the Party should know—is guided by the instructions, the initiative and the leadership of Comrade Stalin. The decision of all important problems of international policy is guided by his recommendations. And not only important problems, but even what might seem third-rate, and even tenth-rate problems interest him, if they affect the workers, the peasants, the laboring people generally of our country.

This, I must say, is true not only of the construction of Socialism in general, but even of the detailed problems of our work. If we take, for example, the defence of our country, it can be quite definitely stated that all the achievements which I have enumerated are solely and entirely due to Stalin.

The powerful will and tremendous organizational talent of this man enables our Party promptly to effect the big historical changes connected with the successful building of Socialism.

[1] S. M. Kirov, speech at the Fifth Leningrad Regional Party Conference, quoted by E. Yaroslavsky, *Landmarks in the Life of Stalin* (Moscow, 1940), p. 185.

1935-36: THE CULT BLOSSOMS

In the mid 1930s, during the first wave of repression which followed the assassination of Kirov, the adulatory tone of public references to Stalin was greatly intensified and the leader's image began to take on divine attributes. The first of the following passages is taken from a speech by the prose-writer A. O. Avdienko to the Seventh Congress of Soviets in February 1935, and the poem appeared in Pravda *in August 1936.*[2]

Thank you, Stalin. Thank you because I am joyful. Thank you because I am well. No matter how old I become, I shall never forget how we received Stalin two days ago. Centuries will pass, and the generations still to come will regard us as the happiest of mortals, as the most fortunate of men, because we lived in the century of centuries, because we were privileged to see Stalin, our inspired leader. Yes, and we regard ourselves as the happiest of mortals because we are the contemporaries of a man who never had an equal in world history.

The men of all ages will call on thy name, which is strong, beautiful, wise and marvellous. Thy name is engraven on every factory, every machine, every place on the earth, and in the hearts of all men.

Every time I have found myself in his presence I have been subjugated by his strength, his charm, his grandeur. I have experienced a great desire to sing, to cry out, to shout with joy and happiness. And now see me—me!—on the same platform where the Great Stalin stood a year ago. In what country, in what part of the world could such a thing happen.

I write books. I am an author. All thanks to thee, O great educator, Stalin. I love a young woman with a renewed love and shall perpetuate myself in my children—all thanks to thee, great educator, Stalin. I shall be eternally happy and joyous, all thanks to thee, great educator, Stalin. Everything belongs to thee, chief of our great country. And when the woman I love presents me with a child the first word it shall utter will be: Stalin.

O great Stalin, O leader of the peoples,
Thou who broughtest man to birth.

[2] *Pravda,* February 1, 1935, and August 28, 1936.

Thou who fructifiest the earth,
Thou who restorest the centuries,
Thou who makest bloom the spring,
Thou who makest vibrate the musical chords . . .
Thou, splendour of my spring, O Thou,
Sun reflected by millions of hearts . . .

1945: THE STAFF OF LIFE

The following verse, taken from a fourth grade school reader published in 1945, is typical of the cult in its mature stage.[3]

Thou, our teacher, like the shining sun,
Dost open my eyes on heaven and earth,
Light up, my sun, shine in my window,
I see in thee the staff of life.

KHRUSHCHEV 1939: "TOWERING GENIUS OF HUMANITY"[4]

From the time of the Yezhovshchina, tributes to Stalin became de rigueur in all public statements by Soviet leaders; these were largely couched in stereotyped phrases, but considerable ingenuity was also displayed in the invention of new titles and attributes. We print here three typical tributes to Stalin by members of his Politburo.

Comrades, we have heard at our Eighteenth Party Congress a report [Stalin's—Ed.] of struggle for communism, the struggle of our workers, peasants and intellectuals, of all the working people of our Soviet land, led by our Party and its Stalinist Central Committee, directed by the genius of our great guide and leader, Comrade Stalin. (*Storm of applause, breaking into an ovation. All rise.*) . . .

The Ukrainian workers and collective farmers are becoming in-

---

[3] From Yanka Kupala, "Stalinu," in *Rodnaia Rech'* (Moscow, 1945), p. 251.

[4] N. S. Khrushchev, Speech to the Eighteenth Congress of the C.P.S.U., in *The Land of Socialism Today and Tomorrow* (Moscow, 1939), pp. 381, 383, 389-90.

creasingly vigilant.[5] We will do our utmost to cultivate these qualities and exterminate like vermin all the foul creatures which the
foreign espionage services furtively deposit on Ukrainian soil. The
Ukrainian people has made havoc of these enemies and traitors,
and rallied closer than ever around the Bolshevik Party and around
our great leader, Comrade Stalin. (*Applause.*) . . .

For many centuries the Ukrainian people fought the tsarist autocracy, the landlords and capitalists. They fought for the right
to develop their native culture, build their own schools, publish
their literature, and study in their mother tongue. And only as a
result of the Great October Socialist Revolution, as a result of
the triumph of the national policy of Lenin and Stalin, as a result
of the special attention paid by Comrade Stalin to the development of Ukrainian culture, have we achieved such momentous
victories in the development of culture.

That is why the Ukrainian people proclaim with all their heart
and soul, with the utmost affection and devotion: "Khai Zhive
Ridny Stalin!" "Long live our beloved Stalin!" (*Thunderous applause, growing to an ovation. All rise. Cheers of* "Long live
Comrade Stalin.") . . .

Comrades! The Eighteenth Party Congress, the historic precepts
of our great Stalin, arm the people of the Soviet Union, arm the
working people of the whole world, with a mighty weapon in the
struggle for communism. Comrade Stalin's doctrine of the socialist
state in a capitalist encirclement,[6] the profound new ideas that
Comrade Stalin's report has introduced into the question of the
Soviet intelligentsia,[7] are a great contribution to the treasure store
of Marxism-Leninism, and mark a *higher stage* in the development
of Leninism.

Long live the friendship of the peoples of the great Soviet Union!
(*Thunderous applause.*)

Long live the Communist Party of the Soviet Union, the party
of the Bolsheviks, the leader and organizer of socialist victory!
(*Applause.*)

Long live the towering genius of all humanity, the teacher and
guide who is leading us victoriously to communism, our beloved

[5] Khrushchev had been Party leader of the Ukraine from January 1938, in the
middle of the *Yezhovshchina*, to which he signifies his full support in this passage. (In 1956 he was to condemn it as a gross abuse of power.)

[6] See above, chapter 2, "The State Under Communism."

[7] See above, chapter 2, "Creating the New Class."

Comrade Stalin! (*Ovation. All rise. Loud cheers of* "Long live our great Stalin.")

BULGANIN 1950: "GREATEST MILITARY LEADER OF MODERN TIMES" [8]

Comrade Stalin has been fighting for the happiness of the working people for over fifty years. His life has been one of self-sacrificing effort, and is an inspiring example for all Soviet people, and for the working people of the whole world.

Comrade Stalin's name is most precious and dear to the heart of all toiling mankind; Stalin is the symbol of all that is advanced and progressive.

Stalin is the genius, the continuer of Lenin's immortal cause, the inspirer and organizer of the building of communism in our country.

Stalin is the creator of the Soviet Armed Forces; he is the greatest military leader of modern times. It was under his guidance that our Armed Forces were created, grew and gained strength. It was under his leadership that they routed the enemy in the period of the Civil War, upheld the freedom and independence of our Motherland in the Great Patriotic War, and saved the peoples of the world from the menace of enslavement to German fascism. Stalin is the creator of the advanced, Soviet military science.

KOSYGIN 1950: "CREATOR OF PARTY, STATE AND ECONOMY" [9]

The establishment of our Communist Party and the first Soviet Socialist State in the world—the symbol of the hopes and aspirations of advanced mankind throughout the world—is indissolubly associated with the name of Stalin.

Comrade Stalin is leading our country along the path indicated by Lenin, along the path of building a communist society. He safeguarded our Bolshevik Party and our state against the enemies of Socialism.

[8] N. Bulganin, *Stalin and the Soviet Armed Forces* (Moscow, 1950), p. 3.

[9] A. Kosygin, *We Are Indebted to the Great Stalin for Our Successes* (Moscow, 1950), pp. 3-4.

Comrade Stalin, the great continuer of Lenin's work, elaborated the plan for the industrialization of the country transforming it, on the basis of the fulfilment of this plan, from a formerly "agrarian and weak country, dependent upon the caprices of the capitalist countries, into an industrial and powerful country."

Comrade Stalin resolutely led our country along the path of building heavy industry, pointing out that heavy industry was the basis of industrialization and of strengthening the country's defence . . .

The most advanced industry in the world, equipped with modern machinery, was built up in our country in an historically short space of time under the leadership of Comrade Stalin. It was Comrade Stalin who showed how best to distribute our industry. . . .

Comrade Stalin displayed his great genius when carrying out Lenin's cooperative plan for the socialist reorganization of the countryside, founded the theory of the collectivization of agriculture. . . .

Directing the entire titantic work of reorganizing our economy, Comrade Stalin guided its development along channels of securing a steady improvement in the material and cultural standard of the working people.

THE CULT SUMMARIZED

The following extracts from Stalin's official biography draw together most of the qualities and achievements attributed to Stalin under the cult. Although this purports to be a sober work of scholarship, it projects an image of superhuman proportions, and is couched in language with marked mythopoeic and even liturgical overtones. For instance, readers versed in Christian symbolism will see here allusions to all three Persons of the Trinity.[10]

Millions of workers from all countries look upon Stalin as their teacher, from whose classic writings they learn how to cope with the class enemy and how to pave the way for the ultimate victory of the proletariat. Stalin's influence is the influence of the

[10] G. F. Alexandrov *et al.*, *Joseph Stalin: A Short Biography* (Moscow, 1947), pp. 198-203.

great and glorious Bolshevik Party, which workers in the capitalist
countries look to as a model to follow, a model of what a working-
class party should be. It was under the leadership of this Party
that capitalism was overthrown and the power of the Soviets, the
power of the working people, established; and under its leadership
that Socialism was built in the U.S.S.R.

The workers of all countries know that every word pronounced
by Stalin is the word of the Soviet people, and that his every word
is followed by action. The triumph of the Socialist Revolution, the
building of Socialism in the U.S.S.R., and the victories of the
Soviet people in their Patriotic War have convinced the laboring
masses of the world of the deep and vital truth of the cause of
Lenin and Stalin. And today the freedom-loving peoples look upon
Stalin as a loyal and staunch champion of peace and security and
of the democratic liberties.

Stalin is the brilliant leader and teacher of the Party, the great
strategist of the Socialist Revolution, military commander, and
guide of the Soviet state. An implacable attitude towards the
enemies of Socialism, profound fidelity to principle, a combination
of clear revolutionary perspective and clarity of purpose with extraordinary firmness and persistence in the pursuit of aims, wise
and practical leadership, and intimate contact with the masses—
such are the characteristic features of Stalin's style. After Lenin,
no other leader in the world has been called upon to direct such
vast masses of workers and peasants. He has a unique faculty for
generalizing the constructive revolutionary experience of the
masses, for seizing upon and developing their initiative, for learning from the masses as well as teaching them, and for leading them
forward to victory.

Stalin's whole career is an example of profound theoretical power
combined with an unusual breadth and versatility of practical experience in the revolutionary struggle.

In conjunction with the tried and tested Leninists who are his
immediate associates, and at the head of the great Bolshevik Party,
Stalin guides the destinies of a multi-national Socialist state, a state
of workers and peasants of which there is no precedent in history.
His advice is taken as a guide to action in all fields of Socialist
construction. His work is extraordinary for its variety; his energy
truly amazing. The range of questions which engage his attention
is immense, embracing complex problems of Marxist-Leninist
theory and school textbooks; problems of Soviet foreign policy and
the municipal affairs of Moscow, the proletarian capital; the de-

velopment of the Great Northern Sea Route and the reclamation of the Colchian marshes; the advancement of Soviet literature and art and the editing of the model rules for collective farms; and, lastly, the solution of most intricate theoretical and practical problems in the science of warfare.

Everybody is familiar with the cogent and invincible force of Stalin's logic, the crystal clarity of his mind, his iron will, his devotion to the party, his ardent faith in the people, and love for the people. Everybody is familiar with his modesty, his simplicity of manner, his consideration for people, and his merciless severity towards enemies of the people. Everybody is familiar with his intolerance of ostentation, of phrasemongers and windbags, of whiners and alarmists. Stalin is wise and deliberate in solving complex political questions where a thorough weighing of pros and cons is required. At the same time, he is a supreme master of bold revolutionary decisions and of swift adaptations to changed conditions.

Stalin is the worthy continuer of the cause of Lenin, or, as it is said in the Party: Stalin is the Lenin of today.

Replying to the congratulations of public bodies and individuals on his fiftieth birthday, in 1929, Stalin wrote: "I set down your congratulations and greetings as addressed to the great Party of the working class, which begot me and reared me in its image. . . . You need have no doubt, comrades, that I am prepared in the future, too, to devote to the cause of the working class, to the cause of the proletarian revolution and world Communism, all my strength, all my faculties, and, if need be, all my blood, to the very last drop."

In the eyes of the peoples of the U.S.S.R., Stalin is the incarnation of their heroism, their love of their country, their patriotism.

With the name of Stalin in their hearts, the working class of the Soviet Union performed unparalleled feats of labor in the Great Patriotic War, supplying the Red Army with first-class weapons and ammunition.

With the name of Stalin in their hearts, the collective farmers toiled devotedly in the fields to supply the Red Army and the cities with food, and industry with raw materials.

With the name of Stalin in their hearts, the Soviet intelligentsia worked with might and main in defence of their country, perfecting the weapons of the Red Army and the technique and organization of industry, and furthering Soviet science and culture.

With the name of Stalin in their hearts, the entire Soviet people are now successfully repairing the damage caused by the war and are striving for a new powerful advance of the Soviet national economy and Soviet culture.

Stalin's name is a symbol of the courage and the renown of the Soviet people, and a call to heroic deeds for the welfare of their great country.

Stalin's name is cherished by the boys and girls of the Socialist land, the Young Pioneers. Their dearest ambition is to be like Lenin and Stalin, to be political figures of the Lenin and Stalin type. . . .

In all their many languages the peoples of the Soviet Union compose songs to Stalin, expressing their boundless devotion for their great leader, teacher, friend and military commander.

In the lore and art of the people, Stalin's name is ever linked with Lenin's. "We go with Stalin as with Lenin, we talk to Stalin as to Lenin; he knows all our inmost thoughts; all his life he has cared for us," runs one of the many Russian folk tales of today.

The name of Stalin is a symbol of the moral and political unity of Soviet society.

With the name of Stalin, all progressive men and women, all the peace-loving democratic nations associate their hope for lasting peace and security.

KHRUSHCHEV 1956:
THE CULT EXPOSED

After Stalin's death, the failure of any of his would-be successors to win a monopoly of supreme power rendered obsolete the whole existing pattern of rule. Neither political police with arbitrary powers nor a leadership cult are consistent with a stable oligarchy. At the same time, the oligarchy sought to strengthen its uncertain position by reducing international tensions and allowing its own people greater freedom and improved living standards. As people grew accustomed to breathing easier and living without a "beloved father and teacher," a flood tide of revulsion set in against all the grayness, fear, and deprivation of the Stalin era. The Soviet Union was rife for "destalinization." It was Khrushchev who seized the opportunity and rode to power on the tide of destalinization, but not before its turbulent waters had almost wrecked him on the reefs of Hungary and Poland. The decisive act, whereby Khrushchev opened the floodgates to destalinization, was his "secret" speech to the Twentieth Congress of the Soviet Communist Party in February 1956, which, as it became known in the months that followed, administered a trauma to the communist movement whose reverberations are still being felt. This speech, however, was important not only for its effects, but for the new information it contained about Stalin's political actions and methods, and about his relations with the members of his entourage. These extracts, therefore, also supplement the reports of individual evaluations of Stalin printed in chapter 4.

Khrushchev begins by referring to Lenin's "testament" (see above, chapter 4, "Lenin: 'Let's Get Rid of Him' ") which had been kept secret in the U.S.S.R. since Lenin's death.[11]

When we analyze the practice of Stalin in regard to the direction of the Party and of the country, when we pause to consider everything which Stalin perpetrated, we must be convinced that Lenin's fears were justified. The negative characteristics of Stalin, which, in Lenin's time, were only incipient, transformed themselves during the last years into a grave abuse of power by Stalin, which caused untold harm to our Party. . . .

He [Stalin—Ed.] discarded the Leninist method of convincing and educating; he abandoned the method of ideological struggle for that of administrative violence, mass repressions, and terror. He acted on an increasingly larger scale and more stubbornly through punitive organs, at the same time often violating all existing norms of morality and of Soviet laws. . . .

Collegiality of leadership flows from the very nature of our Party, a Party built on the principles of democratic centralism. . . .

Whereas during the first few years after Lenin's death Party Congresses and Central Committee plenums took place more or less regularly, later, when Stalin began increasingly to abuse his power, these principles were brutally violated. . . .

Central Committee plenums were hardly ever called. It should be sufficient to mention that during all the years of the Patriotic War not a single Central Committee plenum took place. . . .

[11] From *The Anti-Stalin Campaign and International Communism: A Selection of Documents,* edited by the Russian Institute, Columbia University (New York: Columbia University Press, 1956), pp. 9-10, 14-15, 19, 21-24, 40, 43-45, 50, 52-53, 56-57, 59, 62-64, 69, 77, 80, 82-85. Reprinted by permission of Columbia University Press.

In practice Stalin ignored the norms of Party life and trampled on the Leninist principle of collective Party leadership. . . .

It became apparent that many Party, Soviet and economic activists who were branded in 1937-1938 as "enemies" were actually never enemies, spies, wreckers, etc., but were always honest Communists; they were only so stigmatized, and often, no longer able to bear barbaric tortures, they charged themselves (at the order of the investigative judges—falsifiers) with all kinds of grave and unlikely crimes. . . .

It was determined that of the 139 members and candidates of the Party's Central Committee who were elected at the XVIIth Congress, 98 persons, i.e., 70 per cent, were arrested and shot (mostly in 1937-1938). (*Indignation in the hall.*) . . .

The same fate met not only the Central Committee members but also the majority of the delegates to the XVIIth Party Congress. Of 1966 delegates with either voting or advisory rights, 1108 persons were arrested on charges of anti-revolutionary crimes, i.e., decidedly more than a majority. . . .

This was the result of the abuse of power by Stalin, who began to use mass terror against the Party cadres. . . .

Stalin was a very distrustful man, sickly suspicious; we knew this from our work with him. He could look at a man and say: "Why are your eyes so shifty today," or "Why are you turning so much today and avoiding to look me directly in the eyes?" The sickly suspicion created in him a general distrust even toward eminent Party workers whom he had known for years. Everywhere and in everything he saw "enemies," "two-facers" and "spies."

Possessing unlimited power, he indulged in great willfulness and choked a person morally and physically. A situation was created where one could not express one's own will.

When Stalin said that one or another should be arrested, it was necessary to accept on faith that he was an "enemy of the people.". . .

During the war and after the war Stalin put forward the thesis that the tragedy which our nation experienced in the first part of the war was the result of the "unexpected" attack of the Germans against the Soviet Union. But, Comrades, this is completely untrue. As soon as Hitler came to power in Germany he assigned to himself the task of liquidating Communism. . . .

Documents which have now been published show that by April 3, 1941, Churchill, through his ambassador to the U.S.S.R., Cripps, personally warned Stalin that the Germans had begun regrouping

their armed units with the intent of attacking the Soviet Union.
. . . However, Stalin took no heed of these warnings. What is more,
Stalin ordered that no credence be given to information of this
sort, in order not to provoke the initiation of military operations.

We must assert that information of this sort concerning the
threat of German armed invasion of Soviet territory was coming
in also from our own military and diplomatic sources; however,
because the leadership was conditioned against such information,
such data was dispatched with fear and assessed with reserva-
tion. . . .

Despite these particularly grave warnings, the necessary steps
were not taken to prepare the country properly for defense and
to prevent it from being caught unawares.

It would be incorrect to forget that after the first severe disaster
and defeats at the front, Stalin thought that this was the end. In
one of his speeches in those days he said: "All that which Lenin
created we have lost forever."

After this Stalin for a long time actually did not direct the
military operations and ceased to do anything whatever. He returned to active leadership only when some members of the Political Bureau visited him and told him that it was necessary to take
certain steps immediately in order to improve the situation at the
front.

Therefore, the threatening danger which hung over our Fatherland in the first period of the war was largely due to the faulty
methods of directing the nation and the Party by Stalin himself.

However, we speak not only about the moment when the war
began, which led to serious disorganization of our army and brought
us severe losses. Even after the war began, the nervousness and
hysteria which Stalin demonstrated, interfering with actual military
operations, caused our army serious damage. . . .

Everyone can err, but Stalin considered that he never erred, that
he was always right. He never acknowledged to anyone that he
made any mistake, large or small, despite the fact that he made not
a few mistakes in the matter of theory and in his practical
activity. . . .

Comrades, let us reach for some other facts. The Soviet Union is
justly considered as a model of a multi-national state because we
have in practice assured the equality and friendship of all nations
which live in our great Fatherland.

All the more monstrous are the acts whose initiator was Stalin
and which are rude violations of the basic Leninist principles of the

nationality policy of the Soviet state. We refer to the mass deportations from their native places of whole nations, together with all
Communists and Komsomols without any exception; this deportation action was not dictated by any military considerations. . . .[12]

We must state that after the war the situation became even more
complicated. Stalin became even more capricious, irritable and
brutal; in particular his suspicion grew. His persecution mania
reached unbelievable dimensions. Many workers were becoming
enemies before his very eyes. After the war Stalin separated himself
from the collective even more. Everything was decided by him alone
without any consideration for anyone or anything. . . .

The willfulness of Stalin showed itself not only in decisions concerning the internal life of the country but also in the international
relations of the Soviet Union.

The July Plenum of the Central Committee studied in detail the
reasons for the development of conflict with Yugoslavia. It was a
shameful role which Stalin played here. The "Yugoslav Affair" contained no problems which could not have been solved through
Party discussions among comrades. There was no significant basis
for the development of this "affair"; it was completely possible to
have prevented the rupture of relations with that country. This does
not mean, however, that the Yugoslav leaders did not make mistakes
or did not have shortcomings. But these mistakes and shortcomings
were magnified in a monstrous manner by Stalin, which resulted in
a break of relations with a friendly country.

I recall the first days when the conflict between the Soviet Union
and Yugoslavia began artificially to be blown up. Once, when I
came from Kiev to Moscow, I was invited to visit Stalin who, pointing to the copy of a letter lately sent to Tito, asked me, "Have you
read this?" Not waiting for my reply he answered, "I will shake my
little finger—and there will be no more Tito. He will fall."

We have dearly paid for this "shaking of the little finger." This
statement reflected Stalin's mania for greatness, but he acted just
that way: "I will shake my little finger—and there will be no
Kossior;" "I will shake my little finger once more and Postyshev
and Chubar will be no more;" "I will shake my little finger again

---

[12] Khrushchev is referring here to the brutal wartime deportation of the Bal-
kars, Chechens, Ingushi, Kalmyks, Karachai, Volga Germans, and Crimean Tatars, who were accused of collaboration with the Nazi invaders. Subsequently the
remnants of the first five of these peoples were returned to their homeland, but
the last two remained in exile. See R. Conquest, *The Soviet Deportation of
Nationalities* (London: Macmillan & Co. Ltd., 1960; New York, St. Martin's
Press, 1960).

—and Voznesensky, Kuznetsov and many others will disappear." [13]

Let us also recall the "Affair of the Doctor-Plotters." (*Animation in the hall.*) Actually there was no "Affair" outside of the declaration of the woman doctor Timashuk, who was probably influenced or ordered by someone (after all, she was an unofficial collaborator of the organs of state security) to write Stalin a letter in which she declared that doctors were applying supposedly improper methods of medical treatment.

Such a letter was sufficient for Stalin to reach an immediate conclusion that there were doctor-plotters in the Soviet Union. He issued orders to arrest a group of eminent Soviet medical specialists. He personally issued advice on the conduct of the investigation and the method of interrogation of the arrested persons. He said that the academician Vinogradov should be put in chains, another one should be beaten. Present at this Congress as a delegate is the former Minister of State Security, Comrade Ignatiev. Stalin told him curtly, "If you do not obtain confessions from the doctors we will shorten you by a head." (*Tumult in the hall.*)

Stalin personally called the investigative judge, gave him instructions, advised him on which investigative methods should be used; these methods were simple—beat, beat and, once again, beat.

Shortly after the doctors were arrested we members of the Political Bureau received protocols with the doctors' confessions of guilt. After distributing these protocols Stalin told us, "You are blind like young kittens; what will happen without me? The country will perish because you do not know how to recognize enemies."

The case was so presented that no one could verify the facts on which the investigation was based. There was no possibility of trying to verify facts by contacting those who had made the confessions of guilt. . . .

Comrades! The cult of the individual acquired such monstrous size chiefly because Stalin himself, using all conceivable methods, supported the glorification of his own person. This is supported by numerous facts. One of the most characteristic examples of Stalin's self-glorification and of his lack of even elementary modesty is the edition of his *Short Biography*, which was published in 1948 [see above, chapter 6, "The Cult Summarized"—Ed.] . . . .

Stalin's reluctance to consider life's realities and the fact that he was not aware of the real state of affairs in the provinces can be illustrated by his direction of agriculture. . . .

[13] Kossior, Postyshev, Chubar, Voznesensky, and Kuznetsov were erstwhile lieutenants of Stalin arrested during the 1930s and 1940s.

He knew the country and agriculture only from films. And these films had dressed up and beautified the existing situation in agriculture.

Many films so pictured kolkhoz life that the tables were bending from the weight of turkeys and geese. Evidently Stalin thought that it was actually so. . . .

Stalin separated himself from the people and never went anywhere. This lasted tens of years. The last time he visited a village was in January 1928 when he visited Siberia in connection with grain deliveries. How then could he have known the situation in the provinces? . . .

If we are to consider this matter as Marxists and as Leninists, then we have to state unequivocally that the leadership practice which came into being during the last years of Stalin's life became a serious obstacle in the path of Soviet social development.

Stalin often failed for months to take up some unusually important problems concerning the life of the Party and of the state whose solution could not be postponed. During Stalin's leadership our peaceful relations with other nations were often threatened, because one-man decisions could cause and often did cause great complications. . . .

In the situation which then prevailed I have talked often with Nikolai Alexandrovich Bulganin; once when we two were traveling in a car, he said, "It has happened sometimes that a man goes to Stalin on his invitation as a friend. And when he sits with Stalin, he does not know where he will be sent next, home or to jail."

It is clear that such conditions put every member of the Political Bureau in a very difficult situation. . . .

The importance of the Central Committee's Political Bureau was reduced and its work was disorganized by the creation within the Political Bureau of various commissions—the so-called "quintets," "sextets," "septets" and "novenaries."

One of the oldest members of our Party, Kliment Yefremovich Voroshilov, found himself in an almost impossible situation. For several years he was actually deprived of the right of participation in Political Bureau sessions. Stalin forbade him to attend the Political Bureau sessions and to receive documents. When the Political Bureau was in session and Comrade Voroshilov heard about it, he telephoned each time and asked whether he would be allowed to attend. Sometimes Stalin permitted it, but always showed his dissatisfaction. Because of his extreme suspicion, Stalin toyed also with the absurd and ridiculous suspicion that Voroshilov was an English agent. (*Laughter in the hall.*) It's true—an English agent. A special tapping device was installed in his home to listen to what was said there. (*Indignation in the hall.*)

By unilateral decision Stalin had also separated one other man from the work of the Political Bureau—Andrei Andreyevich Andreyev. This was one of the most unbridled acts of willfulness.

Let us consider the first Central Committee Plenum after the XIXth Party Congress when Stalin, in his talk at the Plenum, characterized Vyacheslav Mikhailovich Molotov and Anastas Ivanovich Mikoyan and suggested that these old workers of our Party were guilty of some baseless charges. It is not excluded that had Stalin remained at the helm for another several months, Comrades Molotov and Mikoyan would probably have not delivered any speeches at this Congress.

Stalin evidently had plans to finish off the old members of the Political Bureau. He often stated that Political Bureau members should be replaced by new ones.

His proposal, after the XIXth Congress [October 1952—ED.], concerning the selection of 25 persons to the Central Committee Presidium, was aimed at the removal of the old Political Bureau members and the bringing in of less experienced persons so that these would extol him in all sorts of ways.

We can assume that this was also a design for the future annihilation of the old Political Bureau members and in this way a cover for all shameful acts of Stalin, acts which we are now considering.

CENTRAL COMMITTEE 1956:
FOR AND AGAINST

In an attempt to contain the effects of destalinization by dissociating the faults of Stalin from the "positive achievements" of the Stalin era, the Soviet Central Committee issued a lengthy statement in June 1956 entitled "On Overcoming the Cult of Personality and its Consequences." This statement also popularized and hallowed the phrase "cult of personality" as the standard euphemism for all the negative features of the Stalin era, a euphemism which became so entrenched that in the mid 1960s Soviet intellectuals continued to label as kultists colleagues accused of dogmatism, obscurantism, repressive methods, or dishonesty.[14] The extracts printed below indicate the balance of black and white contained in this statement, a balance which, with minor fluctuations one way or the other, remained typical of official Soviet evaluations of Stalin throughout the ensuing decade. Thus did the shadow of Stalin hang over the Soviet conscience more than a decade after his death.[15]

Holding the position of General Secretary of the Central Committee of the Party for a lengthy period, J. V. Stalin, together with other leaders, struggled actively for the realization of Lenin's behests. He was devoted to Marxism-Leninism and, as a theoretician and a good organizer, headed the struggle of the party against the Trotskyites, right-wing opportunists, bourgeois nationalists, and against the intrigues of the capitalist encirclement. In this political and ideological struggle Stalin acquired great authority and popularity. However, all our great victories began to be incorrectly connected with his name. The successes attained by the Communist Party and the Soviet country and the adulation of Stalin went to his head. In this atmosphere the cult of Stalin's person began gradually to take shape.

The development of the cult of personality was to an enormous extent contributed to by certain individual traits of J. V. Stalin, the negative character of which was already pointed out by V. I. Lenin. . . .

Having remained at the post of General Secretary of the Central Committee, Stalin, in the first period after Vladimir Ilyich's death, took into account his critical remarks. Later on, however, Stalin, having excessively overrated his merits, came to believe in his own infallibility. He began making some of the limitations on Party and Soviet democracy—unavoidable in conditions of a bitter struggle against the class enemy and its agents and, subsequently, during the war against the German fascist invaders—the norm of intra-Party and state life, riding roughshod over the Leninist principles of leadership. Plenary sessions of the Central Committee and congresses of the Party were held irregularly, and later they were not convened at all for many years. In fact, Stalin became above criticism.

Great harm to the cause of socialist construction, and to the development of democracy inside the Party and the state, was inflicted

[14] See, for instance, Kurt Marko, "History and the Historians," *Survey: A Journal of Soviet and East European Studies*, No. 56 (July 1965), p. 75.

[15] "O preodolenii kul'ta lichnosti i ego posledstvii: Postanovlenie tsentral'nogo komiteta KPSS, 30 iiunia 1956 g.," *Pravda*, July 2, 1956.

by Stalin's erroneous formula that, allegedly, with the advancement of the Soviet Union toward socialism, the class struggle would become more and more acute [see above, chapter 2, "The State Under Communism"—ED.]. . . . In practice, this erroneous theoretical formula was the basis for the grossest violations of socialist law and for mass repressions.

LENIN 1961:
"PLEASE TAKE HIM AWAY"

Subsequently, differing assessments of Stalin and his legacy became one of the central issues in terms of which the emergent differences in the international communist movement, particularly those between the U.S.S.R. and China, were verbalized. At the Twenty-Second Congress of the Soviet Communist Party in October 1961, when these differences were coming to a head, Khrushchev returned to the attack on Stalin, and the delegates witnessed a remarkable speech by D. A. Lazurkina, a party member since 1902, who had suffered years of forced labor at the hands of Stalin, and who told how Lenin had come to her in a vision and had expressed his distaste at having Stalin lying beside him in the Red Square Mausoleum. The Soviet leaders hastened to fulfill this posthumous behest of Lenin. We print here an extract from Lazurkina's speech and the official decision on what since 1953 had been known as "the Mausoleum of Lenin and Stalin." History was taking its vengeance.[16]

Comrades, when we get to our localities we will have to tell the truth honestly, as Lenin taught us to, tell the truth to the workers and the people, about what happened at the congress and what was talked about. And it would be incomprehensible, after what has been said and revealed at the congress, if Stalin were left side by side with Ilyich [Lenin—ED.].

I always carry Ilyich in my heart, always, comrades, and at the most difficult moments the only thing that carried me through was that I had Ilyich in my heart, and could consult with him as to what I must do. (*Applause.*) I consulted with Ilyich yesterday, it

[16] Both selections from *Pravda*, October 31, 1961.

was as if he were alive and standing in front of me, and he said, "It is unpleasant for me to be side by side with Stalin, who brought so many troubles upon the party." *(Stormy and prolonged applause.)*

1961: DECISION OF THE TWENTY-SECOND CONGRESS OF THE C.P.S.U.

On the Mausoleum of Vladimir Ilyich LENIN

1. The Mausoleum in Red Square by the Kremlin wall, created to perpetuate the memory of Vladimir Ilyich LENIN, the immortal founder of the Communist Party and the Soviet state, the leader and teacher of the working people of the whole world, is henceforth to be known as:

The Mausoleum of Vladimir Ilyich LENIN

2. It is acknowledged as inappropriate to retain the sarcophagus containing the coffin of I. V. Stalin in the Mausoleum any longer, since Stalin's serious violations of the behests of Lenin, his abuse of power, his mass repressions against honest Soviet people, and other actions in the period of the cult of personality make it impossible to leave the coffin with his body in the Mausoleum of V. I. Lenin.

CHINA 1963: "A GREAT REVOLUTIONARY"

While Stalin has been removed from the communist pantheon in the U.S.S.R. and in most of the international communist movement, he continues to be honored in China, Albania, and a dozen or so other communist parties aligned with Peking. This divergence in the evaluation of Stalin is linked with a dichotomizing of the communist movement into a more rational, sophisticated, predominantly European wing oriented toward economic effort which is opposed to a more bigoted, crudely ideological, predominantly Asian wing oriented toward political effort. Peking, which has its own leadership cult, requires Stalin as a link in the apostolic succession of Marx-Engels-Lenin-Stalin-Mao. At the same time, it is essential that his image should not dwarf Mao's and that the right of Mao's China to pontificate on his faults and achievements be asserted.

*This is the background to the authoritative Chinese statement
"On the Question of Stalin," excerpted below.*[17]

The Communist Party of China has invariably insisted on an
overall, objective and scientific analysis of Stalin's merits and de-
merits by the method of historical materialism and the presentation
of history as it actually occurred, and has opposed the subjective,
crude and complete negation of Stalin by the method of historical
idealism and the wilful distortion and alteration of history.

The Communist Party of China has consistently held that Stalin
did commit errors, which had their ideological as well as social and
historical roots. It is necessary to criticize the errors Stalin actually
committed, not those groundlessly attributed to him, and to do so
from a correct stand and with correct methods. But we have consistently opposed improper criticism of Stalin, made from a wrong
stand and with wrong methods.

Stalin fought tsarism and propagated Marxism during Lenin's
lifetime; after he became a member of the Central Committee of
the Bolshevik Party headed by Lenin he took part in the struggle
to pave the way for the 1917 Revolution; after the October Revolution he fought to defend the fruits of the proletarian revolution.

Stalin led the CPSU and the Soviet people, after Lenin's death, in
resolutely fighting both internal and external foes, and in safeguard-
ing and consolidating the first socialist state in the world.

Stalin led the CPSU and the Soviet people in upholding the line
of socialist industrialization and agricultural collectivization and
in achieving great successes in socialist transformation and socialist
construction.

Stalin led the CPSU, the Soviet people and the Soviet Army in an
arduous and bitter struggle to the great victory of the anti-Fascist
war.

Stalin defended and developed Marxism-Leninism in the fight
against various kinds of opportunism, against the enemies of Leninism, the Trotskyites, Zinovievites, Bukharinites and other bourgeois agents.

Stalin made an indelible contribution to the international communist movement in a number of theoretical writings which are
immortal Marxist-Leninist works.

[17] *On The Question of Stalin: Comment on the Open Letter of the Central
Committee of the CPSU (II)* (Peking, 1963), pp. 4-19. The statement originally
appeared in *People's Daily* and *Red Flag* (Peking) on September 13, 1963.

Stalin led the Soviet Party and Government in pursuing a foreign policy which on the whole was in keeping with proletarian internationalism and in greatly assisting the revolutionary struggles of all peoples, including the Chinese people.

Stalin stood in the forefront of the tide of history guiding the struggle, and was an irreconcilable enemy of the imperialists and all reactionaries.

Stalin's activities were intimately bound up with the struggles of the great CPSU and the great Soviet people and inseparable from the revolutionary struggles of the people of the whole world.

Stalin's life was that of a great Marxist-Leninist, a great proletarian revolutionary.

It is true that while he performed meritorious deeds for the Soviet people and the international communist movement, Stalin, a great Marxist-Leninist and proletarian revolutionary, also made certain mistakes. Some were errors of principle and some were errors made in the course of practical work; some could have been avoided and some were scarcely avoidable at a time when the dictatorship of the proletariat had no precedent to go by.

In his way of thinking, Stalin departed from dialectical materialism and fell into metaphysics and subjectivism on certain questions and consequently he was sometimes divorced from reality and from the masses. In struggles inside as well as outside the Party, on certain occasions and on certain questions he confused two types of contradictions which are different in nature, contradictions between ourselves and the enemy and contradictions among the people, and also confused the different methods needed in handling them. In the work led by Stalin of suppressing the counter-revolution, many counter-revolutionaries deserving punishment were duly punished, but at the sime time there were innocent people who were wrongly convicted; and in 1937 and 1938 there occurred the error of enlarging the scope of the suppression of counter-revolutionaries. In the matter of Party and government organization, he did not fully apply proletarian democratic centralism and, to some extent, violated it. In handling relations with fraternal Parties and countries, he made some mistakes. He also gave some bad counsel in the international communist movement. These mistakes caused some losses to the Soviet Union and the international communist movement.

Stalin's merits and mistakes are matters of historical, objective reality. A comparison of the two shows that his merits outweighed his faults. He was primarily correct, and his faults were secondary. In summing up Stalin's thinking and his work in their totality, surely every honest Communist with a respect for history will first observe what was primary in Stalin. Therefore, when Stalin's errors are being correctly appraised, criticized and overcome, it is necessary to safeguard what was primary in Stalin's life, to safeguard Marxism-Leninism which he defended and developed.

STALIN IN HISTORY

We are still too close to Stalin to expect to reach a definitive evaluation of his place in history. The four assessments offered in Part Three, therefore, must be regarded as provisional, as soundings in a sea whose general contours remain uncertain.

The impulse behind these soundings is varied. E. H. Carr, having reached the mid 1920s in his monumental multi-volume history of Soviet Russia, found it necessary to sketch in the significance of Stalin as a factor in that history. George F. Kennan experienced the same need in recounting the history of Soviet foreign policy. Robert H. McNeal, convinced of the inadequacy of the evaluation of Stalin by Trotsky, whose misleading influence he detected in such important writings on Stalin as those of Mr. Carr and Mr. Deutscher, approached his own study of Stalin by way of a critical assessment of Trotsky's position. Robert C. Tucker's contribution is in a different genre again: reassessment of the Stalin era, written to serve as a basis for evaluating the changes since Stalin.

All four essays, therefore, approach the problem of Stalin obliquely, though from different directions. They are thus in large measure complementary. Nonetheless, there are also important areas of overlap, and here the reader will find both points of unanimity and points of divergence. Armed with the impressions formed from previous chapters, he will now be in a position to consider these divergencies critically, and to form at least tentative conclusions of his own.

7
E. H. Carr:
"A Great Agent of History"[1]

More than almost any other great man in history, Stalin illustrates the thesis that circumstances make the man, not the man the circumstances. Stalin is the most impersonal of great historical figures. In the party struggles of the nineteen-twenties he appears not to mould events, but to mould himself to them. It is as difficult to define his opinions as to describe his personality. Lack of definition, rather than the shiftiness of which he was often accused, was the distinguishing feature of his position. The claim to be nothing more than a faithful follower and disciple of Lenin was not altogether a pose. He had no creed of his own. He was content to be the favourite son of the revolution and the man of the moment. But this only makes his peculiar personal qualities the more significant. For the qualities which raised him to greatness were precisely the qualities which mirrored the current stage of the historical process. They were the qualities, not only of the man, but of the period. "Every period has its great men," quoted Trotsky from Helvetius, "and if there are none it invents them."[2]

Two characteristic features of Stalin's outlook, both of which reflected his personal background and upbringing, were also con-

---

[1] From E. H. Carr, *Socialism in One Country 1924-1926*, I (New York: The Macmillan Company; London: Macmillan & Co. Ltd., 1958), 176-86. Copyright © 1958 by Edward Hallett Carr. Reprinted by permission of the author and publishers. The pagination is that of the English edition.

[2] L. Trotsky, *Chto i Kak Proizoshlo* (Paris, 1929), p. 26. Later Trotsky offered a more restricted interpretation: "Stalin took possession of power, not with the aid of personal qualities, but with the aid of an impersonal machine. And it was not he who created the machine, but the machine that created him" [see above, chapter 6, "Trotsky 1940: 'The Machine Boss' "—ED.]. But it required something more than a machine to "create" Stalin and put him in power.

spicuous landmarks in the history of the revolution in the middle
nineteen-twenties. The first was a reaction against the predominantly
"European" framework in which the revolution had hitherto been
cast, and a conscious or unconscious reversion to Russian national
traditions. The second was a turning away from the highly developed intellectual and theoretical approach of the first years of the
revolution, and a renewed emphasis on the practical and empirical
tasks of administration. This new attitude had set in after the introduction of NEP, and was well established at the time of Lenin's
death. It was altogether appropriate that the major political figure
of the ensuing period should have been a man with few claims as a
thinker, but an outstanding organizer and administrator.

The absence of any significant western influence in the formation
of Stalin's mind and character distinguished him sharply from the
other early Bolshevik leaders. Alone among them he had never lived
in western Europe, and neither read nor spoke any western language. This peculiarity coloured his personal relations as well as
his political opinions. He never seems to have felt entirely at ease
with colleagues steeped in a European tradition and outlook: he
particularly detested Chicherin and, according to Trotsky,[3] Rakovsky—both of them outstanding representatives of western culture.
Those who stood closest to Stalin in later years—Molotov, Kirov,
Kaganovich, Voroshilov, Kuibyshev—were as innocent as himself of
any western background. Symptoms of a reaction against current
assumptions of European preeminence might have been detected
in Stalin even before the October revolution. When in August 1917
he observed at the sixth party congress in Petrograd that "it would
be unworthy pedantry to ask that Russia should 'wait' with her socialist transformation till Europe 'begins' ", Stalin was merely re-
formulating an idea first propounded by Trotsky and endorsed by
Lenin. But, when he went on to speculate on the possibility that
"Russia may be the country which points the way to socialism", a
new note of national fervour, unfamiliar at this time in Bolshevik
doctrine, was added to the socialist creed.[4] Stalin remained a national rather than an international socialist. In the days when Comintern seemed a living organism, and engaged the constant and
anxious attention of Lenin, Trotsky and Zinoviev, he remained

---

[3] Note on Rakovsky preserved in the Trotsky archives, where Rakovsky as
"a genuine European" is contrasted with Stalin who "most fully represents the
Petrine, most primitive, tendency in Bolshevism."

[4] See E. H. Carr, *The Bolshevik Revolution, 1917-1923*, Vol. I, p. 92.

apparently indifferent to it. He turned to it only in 1924 when it had ceased to be a potential instrument of world revolution, and had become a bureaucratic machine capable of impeding or further-ing Soviet policy or his own political designs.⁴ Stalin's scepticism of the imminence of a German revolution, when this was assumed as a matter of course by almost every other leading Bolshevik, was an early example of his prescience.⁵ By 1925, when he began to preach "socialism in one country", his references to world revolution took on a casual and insouciant air which showed how little his heart was in it.

> When international revolution will break out [he remarked early in that year], it is hard to say; but, when it does break out, it will be a decisive factor.

Or again, a few days later:

> The leading proletariat, the proletariat of the west, is the greatest strength and the most faithful, most important ally of our revolution and of our power. But unfortunately the situation is such, and the condition of the revolutionary movement in the advanced capitalist countries such, that the proletariat of the west is not now in a posi-tion to render us direct and decisive help.⁶

Through all the apparent zigzags of Stalin's economic policy be-tween 1923 and 1928, a single straight line was unwaveringly fol-lowed—the determination to make the Soviet Union powerful, and to make it self-sufficient and independent of the west. An unmistaka-ble note of sincerity, often absent from his polemical utterances, was sounded in his denunciation of Sokolnikov for wanting the "Dawesification" of the Soviet Union, and in his own determination to make it "a country which can by its own efforts produce the equipment it requires." ⁷ Stalin could readily adapt his Marxism to

⁵ See E. H. Carr, *The Interregnum, 1923-1924*, p. 187.

⁶ Stalin, *Sochineniia*, vii, 21, 26. *Biulleten' Oppozitsii* (Paris), No. 19, March 1931, p. 15, collected some remarks on this theme alleged to have been made by Stalin during the 1920s: Comintern, he said, "represents nothing and exists only thanks to our support;" of the KPD [The German Communist Party—Ed.]: "They are all tarred with the same brush; there are no revolutionaries among them any more;" to someone who predicted world revolution within 40 or 50 years: "Rev-olution? Perhaps Comintern will make it? Look: it will make no revolution in 90 years."

⁷ Stalin, *Sochineniia*, vii, 355.

a situation in which Marx's predictions of proletarian revolution in advanced capitalist countries had gone radically astray. Unlike Lenin and Trotsky, or even Zinoviev and Bukharin, Stalin cared nothing for what happened in western Europe except in so far as it affected the destinies of his own country. In pursuit of his aims he would imitate the west, borrow from the west, bargain with the west. But everything was weighed in the scales of national policy.

It is, moreover, remarkable that Stalin's outlook, in spite of his Georgian origin, should have been not merely non-western, but distinctively Russian in the narrower sense. It may be, as has often been suggested, that his character displayed some hidden traits of a primitive Georgian tradition. It is more plausible to associate the frequent brutality and ruthlessness of his behaviour with the grinding poverty and harshness of his earliest environment. At a more conscious level, he seems to have reacted strongly against the predominantly Menshevik strain in Georgian social-democracy.[8] Politically, nothing that was Georgian seemed good to him. He was one of the engineers of the forced subjection of Georgia to Bolshevism in 1921, and throughout his career was notoriously opposed to all manifestations of Georgian nationalism. He was the most "Russian" of the early leaders not only in his rejection of the west, but in his low rating of the local nationalisms of the former Russian Empire. He became the protagonist not only of "socialism in one country", but of a socialism built on a predominantly Russian foundation.

The reaction in Stalin's outlook against the intellectual and the theoretical was no less decisive than his reaction against the west, and was not unconnected with it. The tradition of the Russian intelligentsia was closely bound up with western Europe; the familiar charge against it was that it drew its nourishment from foreign sources, and was divorced from the spirit of the Russian people or nation. All the original Bolshevik leaders, except Stalin, were in a sense the heirs or products of the Russian intelligentsia, and took for granted the premisses of nineteenth-century western rationalism. Stalin alone was reared in an educational tradition which was not

---

[8] The statement quoted in *Zaria Vostoka*, the Tiflis party journal, of December 23, 1925 (an extract from which is in the Trotsky archives), from a Tsarist police report, that Stalin had been active in the social-democratic party since 1902, "first as a Menshevik, then as Bolshevik," has no great significance even if it is true. The split occurred only in 1903 and took some time to penetrate local groups; Zhordania, the future Menshevik leader, was for some time the recognized leader of the whole party. It is certain that, from the moment when Stalin became conscious of the fact and implications of the split, he was whole-heartedly a Bolshevik.

only indifferent to western ways of life and thought, but consciously rejected them. The Marxism of the older Bolsheviks included an unconscious assimilation of the western cultural foundations on which Marxism had first arisen. The fundamental assumptions of the enlightenment were never questioned; a basis of rational argument was always presupposed. Stalin's Marxism was imposed on a background totally alien to it, and acquired the character of a formalistic creed rather than of an intellectual conviction. The former seminarist was predisposed to regard faith as a more important virtue than reason.

Stalin's indifference or distrust for fine-drawn intellectual argument was displayed at an early stage of his party career. In 1911, in a letter to a Caucasian comrade, he called Lenin's famous dispute with Bogdanov on the philosophical premisses of Marxism "a storm in a tea-cup". [9] Stalin never allowed doctrine to stand in the way of the demands of common sense. He was among the first of the Bolsheviks, at the fourth party congress in 1906, to support the distribution of land to the peasants. At the sixth congress in July 1917 he supported the thesis that "Russia may be the country which points the way to socialism" with a phrase which was so often repeated that it became a *cliché:*

> There is a dogmatic Marxism and a creative Marxism: I take my stand on the latter.[10]

In the same spirit many years later, defending the policy of "socialism in one country" against an awkward quotation from Engels, he exclaimed that, if Engels were alive to see the present situation, he would only say: "Devil take the old formulae! Long live the victorious revolution of the USSR!" [11] In the long-standing debate between the determinist or "scientific" and voluntarist or "political" aspects of Marxism there was no doubt on which side Stalin would come down. In a curious unpublished draft essay of 1921 he distinguished the objective and subjective sides of "the proletarian movement", identifying the former with the theory, and the latter with the programme, of Marxism, and added that "the sphere of action of strategy and tactics undoubtedly borders on the subjective side of the

[9] Also published in *Zaria Vostoka* (Tiflis), December 23, 1925.

[10] Stalin, *Sochineniia*, iii, 187.

[11] *Ibid.*, vii, 303.

movement".[12] "A stubborn empiricist, devoid of creative imagination", was Trotsky's summing up.[13] From time to time, by way of vindicating his claim to leadership of the party, Stalin found it necessary to appear in the rôle of a theorist. But it was never in doubt that, in Stalin's conception of politics, doctrine was subsidiary to strategy and tactics.

　Distrust of intellectual processes seems to be reflected in Stalin's dislike of democratic procedures. "Power is exercised", he remarked contemptuously in 1918, "not by those who elect and vote, but by those who govern." [14] Railway transport in the civil war had been disorganized by "a multitude of collegiums and revolutionary committees".[15] At the thirteenth party conference in January 1924 he denounced those "intellectuals" who regarded the right to form fractions as a condition of democracy:

> The mass of the party understands democracy as the creation of conditions which guarantee the active participation of members of the party in the work of leading our country. A few intellectuals of the opposition understand it as giving them the possibility of forming a fraction.[16]

And a few months later he contrasted "a formally democratic party" with "a proletarian party united by indissoluble bonds with the masses of the working class".[17] If, in the Politburo and in other bodies where policy was debated, Stalin had the reputation of being a man of few words, and was slow to commit himself to an opinion whether in speech or in writing,[18] his abstention was perhaps prompted not so much by a deliberate and calculated holding back as by a lack both of taste and of aptitude for such forms of expression. What passed for cunning was, at any rate in early days, the product of diffidence. The rise of Stalin was marked by an eclipse of democratic procedures in the party. Decision by discussion, and

[12] *Ibid.*, v, 62-63.

[13] L. Trotsky, *Chto i Kak proizoshlo*, p. 25.

[14] Stalin, *Sochineniia*, iv, 37.

[15] *Ibid.*, iv, 116-117.

[16] *Ibid.*, vi, 40.

[17] *Ibid.*, vi, 226.

[18] B. Bazhanov, *Stalin* (German transl. from French, 1931), pp. 17, 21.

if necessary by vote, in the central committee or in the Politburo was replaced by disciplined unanimity organized through the power of the secretariat. Stalin never had any of that intellectual pleasure in argument which was so marked in Lenin, Trotsky and Bukharin. Nothing that he said or wrote, at any rate after 1917, was divorced from some immediate political purpose. Trotsky wrote of Stalin's "contemptuous attitude towards ideas".[19] Probably apocryphal utterances later attributed to him, such as "One Soviet tractor is worth ten foreign communists" or "How many divisions has the Pope?", were framed to illustrate the low rating of ideological factors in Stalin's picture of the world.

It may well be that this anti-theoretical bias in Stalin affected his personal relations even more than his political opinions. In the first years after 1917 none of the Bolshevik leaders except Lenin appears to have treated Stalin as an important figure. Lenin recognized his outstanding gifts as an administrator and organizer; the others saw only his commonplace and second-rate theoretical equipment. Yet it was a mistake to deduce from this intellectual shortcoming that Stalin had no gift for handling people. When he received a delegation of peasants in March 1925, he seems, from what looks like an authentic contemporary record, to have been remarkably successful in establishing easy relations with them. He "listened attentively like a *muzhik* and puffed at his pipe", commented on practical points and exchanged artless jokes, so that "all were astonished at this simple, comradely attitude of comrade Stalin towards us, comparing it with the roughness and bureaucratic attitude of local party officials to the peasantry".[20] In his dealings with colleagues, this ease of intercourse vanished altogether.[21] It was to them that Stalin exhibited the "rudeness" and lack of "loyalty" of which Lenin complained in the testament. Stalin smarted under their cov-

[19] See above, chapter 5, "Trotsky 1940: 'The Machine Boss' "—ED.

[20] The interview, which took place on March 14, 1925, was reported in *Bednota* (the peasant newspaper), April 5, 1925, by one of the participants; though it shows Stalin in an unusually agreeable light, it was never utilized by any of Stalin's biographers, presumably because it contained an incautious remark about tenure of land which Stalin was afterwards obliged to disown (see E. H. Carr, *Socialism in One Country 1924-1926*, I, 247-48).

[21] One of Demian Bedny's doggerel poems, intended as a friendly caricature, recounted an interview with Stalin at which he made all the correct remarks, while Stalin stroked his moustaches without uttering a single word, till he rose to end the interview with a hearty "Come again—it's pleasant to have a chat" (*Molodaia Gvardiia*, No. 9, September 1925, pp. 205-206).

ert assumption of superiority, and met it with a constant sly depreciation of the party intellectuals. When attacking Trotsky, he recalled that Lenin at the second congress of the party had resisted Martov's demand to open the party to "non-proletarian elements" —an odd distortion of the famous dispute about the party statute— and quoted Lenin's rare criticism of the predominance of intellectuals in the party at the third party congress of 1905.[22] One of the frankest expressions of Stalin's feelings appeared in a letter written to the German Communist Party leader Maslow in 1925:

> We in Russia have also had a dying away of a number of old leaders from among the *littérateurs* and old "chiefs". . . . . This is a necessary process for a renewal of the leading cadres of a living and developing party.

And he named Lunacharsky, Bogdanov, Pokrovsky and Krasin among "former Bolshevik leaders who have passed over to a secondary rôle".[23] Those whom he gathered around himself in later years were for the most part good party men whose theoretical pretensions were as few as his own. One of many interpretations of the great purges of the nineteen-thirties was that they were Stalin's final vengeance on the intellectuals who had despised him. He was particularly ruthless in forcing the intellectual life of the country into a narrow political strait-jacket. "We, Bolshevik practitioners," he was to say in the preface to the collected edition of his works in 1946.[24]

• It has often been suggested that Stalin's background and education are reflected in his literary style. Lenin wrote and spoke plainly and easily with the air of one too completely preoccupied with what he is saying to pay much attention to the way in which it is said. Trotsky displayed the slightly mannered brilliance of an artist in words. Bukharin took evident pleasure, which communicated itself to the reader or hearer, in the lucidity and ingenuity of his argument. Neither the spoken nor the written word seemed to come easily to Stalin. His style had the workmanlike virtues of clarity and precision; its vice was a total lack of imagination or of grace. When he wished to impress, he resorted to the schematic devices of enumeration, repetition and the rhetorical question, in which some

[22] See E. H. Carr, *The Interregnum, 1923-1924*, p. 353.

[23] Stalin, *Sochineniia*, vii, 43.

[24] *Ibid.*, i, p. xiii.

critics detected liturgical echoes. But the form remained stiff, the content intellectually and emotionally trivial. Some of Stalin's earlier speeches made a favourable impression of moderation and caution. The applause that greeted his later denunciations of his enemies to packed audiences was no test. Stalin's victories were not won in the debating-chamber, and there is little evidence that he desired to shine there. The period of revolutionary oratory had passed with the day of the intellectuals.

If, however, Stalin, in his reaction against western influence and in his reaction against a theoretical approach to politics, was the product of his period, the dramatic element in Stalin's career and personality resides in the fact that it was he, above all, who carried forward the revolution to its appointed conclusion by bringing about the rapid industrialization of the country. By the irony of history it was Stalin, and not Trotsky, who became the effective champion of forced industrialization and comprehensive planning, and was prepared to sacrifice the peasant to this overriding purpose. It would be fanciful to ascribe this turn of events to any personal conviction or prejudice on Stalin's part; nor is it necessary to convict him of hypocrisy when he attacked Trotsky for advocating measures less draconian than those which he himself would one day adopt. Nothing could better reveal the essentially impersonal character of Stalinist policy. If Stalin's methods often seemed to reflect characteristics derived from his personal background and upbringing, the aims which he pursued were dictated by the dynamic force inherent in the revolution itself. What Stalin brought to Soviet policy was not originality in conception, but vigour and ruthlessness in execution. When he rose to power in the middle nineteen-twenties, he became, and was determined to remain, the great executor of revolutionary policy. But the course of events makes it clear that he had at that time no vision of where that policy would lead.

Stalin's rôle in history thus remains paradoxical and in some sense contradictory. He carried out, in face of every obstacle and opposition, the industrialization of his country through intensive planning, and thus not only paid tribute to the validity of Marxist theory, but ranged the Soviet Union as an equal partner among the Great Powers of the western world. In virtue of this achievement he takes his undisputed place both as one of the great executors of the Marxist testament and one of the great westernizers in Russian history. Yet this *tour de force* had, when studied and analysed, a supremely paradoxical character. Stalin laid the foundations of the proletarian revolution on the grave of Russian capitalism, but through a deviation from Marxist premisses so sharp as to amount almost to a rejection of them. He westernized Russia, but through a revolt, partly conscious, partly unconscious, against western influence and authority and a reversion to familiar national attitudes and traditions. The goal to be attained and the methods adopted or proposed to attain it often seemed in flagrant contradiction—a contradiction which in turn reflected the uphill struggle to bring a socialist revolution to fruition in a backward environment. Stalin's ambiguous record was an expression of this dilemma. He was an emancipator and a tyrant; a man devoted to a cause, yet a personal dictator; and he consistently displayed a ruthless vigour which issued, on the one hand, in extreme boldness and determination and, on the other, in extreme brutality and indifference to human suffering. The key to these ambiguities cannot be found in the man himself. The initial verdict of those who failed to find in Stalin any notable distinguishing marks had some justification. Few great men have been so conspicuously as Stalin the product of the time and place in which they lived.

8

Robert H. McNeal:
Trotsky's Interpretation
of Stalin[1]

Rarely has the historical image of a major leader been shaped as much by his arch-enemy as the generally accepted conception of Stalin has been shaped by the writings of Trotsky. In some ways this is neither unnatural nor regrettable. Trotsky had unsurpassed direct access to knowledge of Stalin's career between 1917 and 1928 and excellent indirect access to information on the rest of his life. Moreover, Trotsky was, at best, a highly talented biographical and historical writer, worthy of the respect of scholars in a way that the mendacious and heavy-handed Stalin never was. Trotsky's treatment of documents has proven to be scrupulous as far as facts are concerned, and there is a great deal in his interpretation of Stalin that merits high respect. Finally, Stalin's virulent attack upon historical truth and his murderous interruption of Trotsky's biographical work have predisposed non-Soviet writers in Trotsky's favour.[2]

[1] From Robert H. McNeal, "Trotsky's Interpretation of Stalin," in G. S. N. Luckyj (ed.), *Canadian Slavonic Papers*, V (University of Toronto Press, 1961), pp. 87-97. Reprinted, in slightly condensed form, by permission of the author and the editors of *Canadian Slavonic Papers*. For the essentials of Trotsky's interpretation, see chapter 5, "Trotsky 1940: 'The Machine Boss.'"

[2] The two best known English writers on Stalin and his era, E. H. Carr and Isaac Deutscher, appear to accept Trotsky's interpretation of Stalin in very great measure. In his imposing study of Soviet Russia Mr Carr states his thesis on Stalin's place in history by explicitly accepting Trotsky's summation of Stalin in the words of Helvetius, "Every period has its great men, and if there are none it invents them" [see above, chapter 7, "A Great Agent of History"— ED.]. Mr Deutscher, an admirable and highly sympathetic biographer of Trotsky, drew heavily on Trotsky's interpretation in *Stalin: A Political Biography*. However, it would take a separate article to appraise Mr Deutscher's profuse writings related to Stalin and the relationship of his ideas to Trotsky's.

It is pointless to tilt indiscriminately at the entire image of Stalin that Trotsky established. Nor is it enlightening to carp at Trotsky's undoubted prejudice regarding Stalin. It is rather to be wondered that the polemical reaction of a leader so naturally proud and combative as Trotsky was so restrained, considering the provocation that Stalin gave him. But after granting Trotsky his due, it remains desirable to review his interpretation of Stalin and to suggest some of the major and minor points on which one may differ with Trotsky.

One is least likely to disagree with Trotsky concerning Stalin's personal characteristics, for even the hardiest reviser of Trotsky's interpretation would scarcely attempt to portray Stalin as either a moral examplar or an intellectual of great erudition or polished style. But it may justly be said that Trotsky's portrait of a repellent and dull-witted mediocrity is partly beside the point and partly mistaken in fact. One can hardly deny that Stalin was capable of cruelty and deceit in the fullest measure, but this need not lead to Trotsky's conclusion that Stalin was merely a cynical power-seeker, and not a devotee of a messianic ideology. "The mainspring of his personality," Trotsky writes of Stalin, was "love of power, ambition, envy—active never-slumbering envy of all who were more gifted, more powerful, rank higher than he. . . . Psychologically, power to him was always something apart from the purposes which it was supposed to serve. The desire to exert his will as the athlete exerts his muscles, to lord it over others—that was the mainspring of his personality." [3]

The trouble with Trotsky's interpretation is that he mistakes morality, by which he means devotion to Communist ideas, for the prudery that characterized his own expression of ideological fanaticism. The subordination of ends to means, the conviction that one must secure absolute power first and then consider reform, was basic to Lenin and to bolshevism. Stalin and Trotsky shared a ruthless ideology, but Trotsky, the articulate *intelligent,* expressed his conviction in a style that was very unlike Stalin's more plodding, colourless manner. Trotsky himself called attention to the contrast between the two personalities: on one hand the cosmopolitan, puritanical *intelligent,* accustomed to a life of theoretical activity as an *émigré;* on the other hand, the provincial semi-proletarian, given to "pragmatic" or "practical" labours. [4] This psychological gulf

---

[3] See above, chapter 5, "Trotsky 1940: 'The Machine Boss' "—Ed.

[4] Trotsky, *Stalin: An Appraisal of the Man and His Influence* (New York, 1941), pp. 54, 130.

seems to have prevented Trotsky from giving Stalin his due as a true believer. The full measure of Trotsky's holier-than-thou attitude is found in the booklet *Their Morals and Ours,* in which he confidently asserts the immeasurable moral superiority of his own faction over "them"—i.e., all other contemporary political groups.[5] It is not surprising that such a prophet could see only coarse vulgarity in Stalin, and would fondly quote Krupskaya's alleged remark that "he [Stalin] is devoid of the most elementary honesty, the most simple human honesty. . . ." [6]

But this is really beside the point. The mannerisms of the non-*émigré,* non-intellectual Stalin in no way precluded devotion to an intense conception of Communism. Trotsky has only proven that Stalin did not display the more obvious traits that the typically self-righteous, puritanical *intelligent* had shown ever since Chernyshevsky sketched the archetype in Rakhmetov, the hero of *Chto delat'?* In showing this, Trotsky has illuminated himself more than Stalin.

The contrast between their personalities prevented Trotsky from appreciating Stalin's mental powers, just as it constricted his conception of Communist morality. To Trotsky, intellectual capacity meant talent for theoretical treatises and he failed to evaluate justly a comparable quality in Stalin, his good memory. Refuting a Soviet writer on Stalin's success as a seminarist, Trotsky writes: "As a matter of fact, Stalin's memory—at least, his memory for theories—is quite mediocre." [7] Such a statement is a good example of the intellectual bias that hampered Trotsky's appreciation of Stalin, and it may explain why Trotsky refuses to give Stalin credit for the powers of memory that later impressed such anti-Communist observers of the dictator as Philipi Mosely and Vilhelms Munters.[8]

[5] Trotsky, *Their Morals and Ours* (Mexico, 1939).

[6] Trotsky, *Stalin,* p. 375. [Nadezhda Krupskaya was Lenin's wife—ED.] Krupskaya's deep attachment to the traditions of the radical intelligentsia provided her with a viewpoint and emotional responses that were very like Trotsky's. One of the marks of Lenin's unusual stature among the intellectual leaders of the radicals was his capacity to recognize Stalin's immense political talent, despite the latter's crudities. Compare Lenin's early interest in Stalin with Trotsky's tendency to dismiss Stalin as a nullity after the latter supposedly showed coarse amusement at Kollontai's *amour* with the sailor Dybenko [see above, chapter 4, "Trotsky: 'Vulgarity and Animosity' "—ED.].

[7] Trotsky, *Stalin,* p. 110.

[8] P. E. Mosely, "Across the Green Table from Stalin," *Current History,* xv, 85 (1948), 130; Munters' impression cited in Arnold and Veronica Toynbee (eds.), *Survey of International Affairs, 1939-1946: The Initial Triumph of the Axis* (London, 1958), p. 49.

The identification of mental capacity and formal theoretical talent undoubtedly helped to shape Trotsky's low opinion of Stalin's intelligence as a whole. On this issue it is probably safe to say that most witnesses of Stalin at work would disagree with Trotsky's belief that Stalin possessed "a slow intellect," while they would agree that Stalin was a dull orator and writer.[9] The obvious truth of this latter criticism may have helped to deceive Trotsky on the point that he seems to have considered basic concerning Stalin's mentality: his alleged "narrowness of horizon and lack of creative imagination." [10] Again, predilection for the *style* of the cosmopolitan *intelligent* prevented his recognizing good Leninism when he saw it.

As for theory, it is plausible to argue that Stalin's mature doctrinal writings represent an original reinterpretation and extension of Leninism. Although this discussion cannot cope with so large an issue, one can at least observe that Trotsky himself has provided some basis for such an interpretation. Trotsky asserts that Stalin's first well-known essay on the question of minority nationalities, now usually entitled "Marxism and the National Question," is the work of "an outstanding theoretician." [11] After lavishing praise on this essay, Trotsky attempts to demonstrate that it was really Lenin's handiwork. Although this hypothesis has now been widely disseminated, the evidence to the contrary is varied and compelling. One may begin by dismissing Trotsky's notion that the article illustrates Lenin's "trenchant" style. It is as awkward as most of Stalin's prose and includes some phraseology taken directly from an earlier article by Stalin, written *before* Lenin's alleged exercise as a ghost-writer. Moreover, it is hard to disagree with Richard Pipes that textual analysis of the article does not indicate that Lenin dictated it.[12] Nor is it true that Stalin had no ideas on this issue before his discussions with Lenin in 1913. Much of the essence of "Marxism and the National Question" may be found in an article published by Stalin

[9] Compare the evaluations assembled in chapter 5 (ED.).

[10] Trotsky, *The History of the Russian Revolution* (London, 1932), iii, 164. Cf., however, Churchill, speaking of Stalin's reaction to the proposal of Operation Torch: "Very few people alive could have comprehended in so few minutes the reasons which we had all been so busily wrestling with for months. He [Stalin] saw it all in a flash." [See above, chapter 4, "Churchill: 'Deeply Impressed'" —ED.].

[11] Trotsky, *Stalin*, pp. 156-58.

[12] Richard Pipes, *The Formation of the Soviet Union* (Cambridge, 1954), pp. 40-41.

in Georgian in 1904, well before Lenin had given the issue of nationality any systematic attention.[13] Finally, Trotsky contradicts available evidence in asserting that Stalin returned to Cracow, from Vienna, where he wrote the article, thus giving Lenin a chance to revise what was allegedly his own creation in the first place. There is in fact no evidence that Stalin saw Lenin on the return trip or that Lenin read the manuscript before it went to press.[14]

The expenditure of some effort to undermine Trotsky's thesis that Stalin did not contribute much to the composition of "Marxism and the National Question" is worth while if one remembers that Trotsky was so enthusiastic in his praise of this article. If Stalin was essentially its author, even with initial encouragement from Lenin, then Trotsky should be prepared to admit that Stalin was capable of original and penetrating theoretical work, and the crux of his deprecation of Stalin's intelligence collapses. In short, Trotsky's interpretation of Stalin's character and talents is inadequate, the most serious distortions resulting not so much from political animus as from the blind spots in the make-up of the radical *intelligent*, whom Trotsky typified.

In his interpretation of the success of Stalin and the nature of Stalinist Russia, Trotsky's approach was complicated by his commitment to a Marxist conception of the historical process, his deep sense of association with the party, and his acceptance of some of the important policies of Stalinism. However much he was impelled to condemn Stalinism, he was reluctant to abandon his faith in the proletarian revolution as the gateway to the Communist utopia.

Because Trotsky was an especially theoretically-minded Marxist, an examination of his attempted resolution of this dilemma must begin with the theory of history and society. The main point here is that Trotsky could not bring himself to admit that Stalinism was the "scientifically" predicted fulfilment of the proletarian revolution or that Marxism was erroneous at base.[15] And this unwill-

[13] Stalin, *Sochineniia*, I, 32-55.

[14] Neither the Stalinist sources, such as the biographical chronicle in his *Sochineniia* (Collected Works), nor independent sources, such as Krupskaya's recollections, refer to any visit by Stalin *en route* from Vienna to St Petersburg in 1913. Stalin was sufficiently eager to exaggerate his personal connection with Lenin that such a visit, had there been one, would surely have been noted.

[15] He specifically denied that Stalin was the "legitimate" (*zakonnyi*, meaning ordained by natural law in this instance) product of Bolshevism. "Stalinism and Bolshevism" (New York, 1937).

ingness to accept either unpalatable solution to his dilemma led him to construct a somewhat tortuous explanation of Soviet Russian history. At the heart of Trotsky's apologia on behalf of Russian history is the well-known analogy with the French Revolution, its relapse from the intense reforming spirit of the Jacobins to the lax and even counter-revolutionary periods of the Thermidoreans and Bonapartists. Such a comparison of major revolutions is accepted in some measure by almost all historians, and for Trotsky the theory of a Russian Thermidor had two special attractions: it exonerated the "old" Bolshevik party and the October Revolution of responsibility for Stalinism, and it deprived Stalin of all personal credit for the post-revolutionary development of Soviet Russia, whether meritorious or deplorable. In pressing this argument, Trotsky inveighed against any attempt to assassinate Stalin, holding that the only result would be the succession of another equally competent bureaucrat.[16] Because Trotsky was convinced that Stalin was a mediocrity, he felt that his apparent triumph could only be the work of greater forces.

Although the idea of a Russian Thermidor had strong appeal for Trotsky, his loyalty to Marxism and the Party inhibited his enthusiasm for it. . . . In 1928 he still held that the danger of Thermidor, and Bonapartism as well, was still present, though not yet triumphant, but in 1929 he was sufficiently impressed by the leftward swing of the Stalin régime to drop the matter temporarily. . . .[17] It was only in 1935 after the opening of the purges that Trotsky was ready to acknowledge this victory, and even to acknowledge that it dated back to about 1925.[18] Russia, said Trotsky, had experienced its peculiar kind of Thermidor, which he distinguished from the Thermidor of France, and was in 1935 at the beginning of the Bonapartist era, appoximately analogous to the position of France during the Consulate. Conscious that this argument suggested that Stalin could be identified with Napoleon, an imposing figure even in the eyes of Marxists, Trotsky noted that the parallel was sociological and not personal. Having arrived at this position, Trotsky main-

---

[16] "Doloi Stalina," Trotsky Archives, Harvard College Library, No. 4329.

[17] Trotsky, "What Now?," in *The Third International After Lenin* (New York, 1936).

[18] Trotsky, "Rabochee gosudarstvo, termidor i bonapartizm," *Biulleten' oppozitsii*, No. 43.

tained it in essence in his widely read book of 1936, *The Revolution Betrayed,* and in other writings up to the time of his death.[19]

Trotsky seems to have been satisfied with his theory as it related to Stalin, but he was markedly uncomfortable with the general theoretical consequences that his interpretation of Stalin implied. In explaining Stalin's success as the unavoidable relapse of the post-revolutionary era, Trotsky came close to revising Marxism by the discovery of new, cyclical laws governing the history of man *beyond* the "proletarian" revolution. . . .

But Trotsky was unwilling to sacrifice the optimistic teleology to which he had devoted his life in order to belittle Stalin's achievements. His attempts to show that the laws of history were still benign, even though they produced Stalinism, were rather tortured and scholastic, lacking both the conviction and the insight of the best of his youthful theoretical sallies. . . .

There are also grounds for criticizing Trotsky's belief that the emergence of the Stalinist party signified the triumph of non-revolutionary elements not because of their leader's ability but because of the "dialectics of history," which "hooked onto him" and "raised him up." According to Trotsky, Stalin's *politburo* was composed chiefly of career-seeking nonentities, and the imposition of undiluted discipline in the party was the attempt of this bureaucracy to eliminate the true Communists. His own attachment to the social type of the *intelligent* and the *émigré* radical seems to have warped his interpretation of this point. It is true that Stalin's inner circle included mainly non-*intelligent* Communists like Stalin, but in the Five-Year Plans Stalin and his lieutenants conducted a revolutionary economic policy that satisfied Trotsky's main desiderata: rapid industrialization, collectivization of agriculture, and state planning. However much he criticized the administrative bungling of Stalin's economic system, Trotsky acknowledged that the main direction of the economy had been progressive.[20] But how could the leaders who seemed to be responsible for such policies be Thermidoreans or Bonapartists? Trotsky attempted to resolve this dilemma by representing Stalin as "an opportunist with a bomb," who merely reacted

---

[19] Trotsky, "Pochemu Stalin pobedil oppozitsiiu?," *Biulleten' oppozitsii,* No. 46; *The Revolution Betrayed* (London, 1937); "Termidor i anti-semitizm," Archives No. 4106; *Stalin* [extracts in chapter 5, above—ED.].

[20] Trotsky, "Rabochee gosudarstvo, termidor i bonapartizm," *The Revolution Betrayed,* pp. 9, 43, 48; "SSSR v voine."

to external pressures in conducting the drastic programme of the early Five-Year Plans. Trotsky's thesis, which has been widely accepted, holds that the stalemate between agriculture and industry, which reached a high point in 1928, forced Stalin's hand.[21] There are economic arguments against the view that massive collectivization was the only course open to Stalin, as Professor Alec Nove recently pointed out in a critique of E. H. Carr's treatment of the subject.[22] So far, no thorough economic study of Stalin's régime has done justice to the alternatives, and this paper can only allude to so complex a question. But on non-technical grounds it may be argued that no radical, risky attempt at solution need be expected from a mere opportunist or even from the normal run of politicians. Trotsky attempted to brush off Stalin's immense act of will in the first Five-Year Plan as "opportunism . . . turned into its opposite, adventurism," but such dialectical word-play does not explain much.[23]

Basic to all of Trotsky's criticism of Stalin is the well-known issue of international revolution. According to Trotsky, a vicious circle frustrated the proletariat. The delay of widespread proletarian revolution made possible the conditions in Russia that brought Stalin to power, and Stalin did all he could to oppose the world revolution that would spell his own doom.[24] Trotsky was successful in convincing a multitude of listeners, including some western diplomats, of this point. No doubt he was assisted by Stalin, who spoke of "socialism in one country" and, to Trotsky's delight, told Roy Howard that talk of Soviet support of international revolution was a "tragi-comic error." [25]

---

[21] *The Revolution Betrayed*, p. 38 ff.

[22] Alec Nove, "The Peasants, Collectivization and Mr Carr," *Soviet Studies*, x, 4 (1959), pp. 384-89.

[23] Trotsky, *The Revolution Betrayed*, p. 41. Mr Deutscher in *The Prophet Unarmed*, p. 466, asserts that "Trotsky was the authentic inspirer of the second revolution of which Stalin was to be the manager . . ." This judgment justifies Trotsky's hopes that the opposition could turn a temporary left swing of the régime into a firm policy (e.g. "What Now?" p. 289 ff.). But it seems to this writer that Trotsky's encouragement was about the last influence that would have decided Stalin in favour of any policy.

[24] Among many examples see "Rabochee gosudarstvo, termidor i bonapartizm;" *The Revolution Betrayed*, p. 263; Archives, No. 4204; "Gitler i Stalin."

[25] Trotsky, "Zaiavlenie i otkrovenie Stalina," Archives, No. 3903. The text of the Stalin interview with Howard appears in *Pravda*, March 5, 1936.

But Stalin never spoke of socialism in one country as more than a temporary necessity and in contrast to his words to Howard, a foreign publicist, he maintained to the Party that the USSR was to be a base for international revolution. When the Nazi-Soviet Pact of 1939 was signed, Trotsky sarcastically wrote, "And there are people who still assert that the end of the present Kremlin is international revolution." [26] But even before Trotsky's murder, Stalin had exploited the pact to Communize a wide swath in Eastern Europe.

Trotsky allowed himself to be led astray by the verbal differences that separated him from Stalin on the issue of world revolution—a natural error considering that Stalin made a fetish of several doctrinal formulations on this subject. But both men held the axiom that Communism could be secure only in a largely Communist world. Both believed in using the resources of the USSR to this end, without sacrificing the one bastion of Communism in any futile adventurism. Differences on specific tactics, and especially in the use of the Comintern, were real and intense, but Trotsky and Stalin were equally wrong in leaping from these conflicts to the conclusion that the other had betrayed international revolution.

A final measure of Trotsky's misjudgment of Stalin and his works is the conviction that neither could survive for long. Convinced that his own time was running out,[27] Trotsky insisted that Stalin's fate was sealed, especially with the coming of the war, which Trotsky correctly foresaw. In an article about the expected war Trotsky rhetorically asked, "Can there be the least doubt about the fate that awaits him [Stalin]?" [28] So certain was he that the Stalinist structure was near collapse that he renounced the one plan that might have offered his faction some rational hope. That is, Trotsky refused to repeat the Leninist slogans of 1917 and adopt a "defeatist" policy toward Russia. Instead, he took a line rather like the ambiguous one that Stalin had once taken towards the Provisional Government. We will defend the USSR, said Trotsky, but not the Stalinist government. Its defense is the defense of the revolution; "we do not concede to Hitler the overthrowing of Stalin; that is *our task*." [29] At this point Trotsky's refusal to face the truth about Stalin led him very far

---

[26] Trotsky, "Stalin, intendant Gitlera," Archives, No. 4612.

[27] *Trotsky's Diary in Exile 1935*, pp. 165-66.

[28] E.g. Trotsky, "Svezhii urok (k voprosu o kharaktere predstoiashchei voiny," *Biulleten' oppozitsii*, No. 71 (October, 1938).

[29] Trotsky, "SSSR v voine."

from reality, for the Fourth International was in no position to "defend" or "overthrow" anyone. Having lost hope that the Communist Party of the Soviet Union could be saved, Trotsky clung to the unjustified hope that the masses in Russia remained true to the cause and that history was still for Trotsky and against Stalin. To the end of his life he could not believe that so vulgar a person as Stalin was capable of the most staggering social and economic undertakings or that "history" could continue to suffer such a creature.

9

Robert C. Tucker:
"A Twentieth-Century
Ivan the Terrible"[1]

The Bolshevik seizure of power in October 1917, followed by the establishment of a one-party dictatorship and the nationalization of the Russian economy, destroyed the democratic regime that had been set up some months earlier when the Czar abdicated. It also nullified the previous sixty-five years of Russian history, during which, despite many setbacks, a trend of basic liberalization had been making itself felt. The Revolution thus created conditions for a reversion to that long period in Russian history which had been characterized by the ascendancy of the state over society, and by government through bureaucracy, with the Czar as head bureaucrat. Bolshevism set the stage for a rebirth, under a new name and in a far worse form, of the classical political system of Russian czarism as it had existed before the great reforms of the mid-nineteenth century.

It was Stalin, however, not Lenin, who made himself the key instrument of this process and restored the institution of the autocracy in all but name. In the later years of Stalin's rule, Czar Ivan the Terrible, the supreme historical apostle of Russian absolutism, became the dictator's favorite figure among those whom he regarded as his forerunners. In 1947, Stalin called in a famous Soviet film producer and ordered him to make a film showing Ivan as a "great and wise ruler." He commented that, of all the leaders in Russian

[1] From Robert C. Tucker, *The Soviet Political Mind: Studies in Stalinism and Post-Stalin Change* (New York: Frederick A. Praeger, Inc.; London and Dunmow, Pall Mall Press, 1963), pp. 37-38, 40-53. Originally published as "The Politics of Soviet De-Stalinization," *World Politics*, IX: 4 (July 1957). Reprinted by permission of the author, the RAND Corporation, Frederick A. Praeger, Inc., and the editors of *World Politics*.

history, Ivan and Lenin were the only two who had introduced a
state monopoly of foreign trade.[2] This remark indicates the nature
of Stalin's understanding of socialism. It did not seem to him an
ideological deviation to look upon Ivan the Terrible as his great
historical forerunner. He saw in Ivan a true socialist, a Stalinist of
the sixteenth century. This fact is full of implications for an understanding of Soviet Russia's history in the Stalin period, and of the
events that followed.

The governmental system as Stalin left it might be described as an
elaborate, completely centralized bureaucratic mechanism for the
command and control of society. The centralization of effective governing authority in Moscow was so extreme that semi-official Soviet
idiom divided the whole Soviet realm into the "Center" (Moscow)
and the "Periphery" (all the rest of the USSR). For example, a high
official of the theoretically sovereign government of the Ukraine at
Kiev informally described himself as "a worker of the Periphery."
This was the actual situation behind the façade of Soviet "federal-
ism," according to which the USSR consists of a number of independent "union republics." . . .

There are three main systems of governing organs: (1) the Soviets,
forming the nominal machinery of local government, plus the Supreme Soviet, a facsimile of a parliament; (2) the system of minis-
tries, subordinated to the Council of Ministers of the USSR, which is
the government in the technical sense; and (3) the Communist
Party, headed up by its Central Committee. . . .

This great bureaucratic structure of command and control did
not come into being all at once; it evolved. The October Revolution
and Lenin's party dictatorship laid the foundation and paved the
way. But the evolution itself took place under the direction and pre-
eminent influence of Stalin. . . .

Stalin, using the party dictatorship, of which he had gained control by about 1929, and the secret police, which he increasingly succeeded in wielding as a personal instrument, ended the NEP and
then shaped, perfected, and vastly expanded the command and control structure. His idea was to effect in this manner the total state
regimentation of society, creating in the totalitarian political structure a mechanism for unlimited exploitation of the human and
natural resources of Russia with a view to amassing power in the
hands of the Center. The forced industrialization, beginning with
the First Five-Year Plan in 1928, and the terroristic collectivization

[2] S. M. Dubrovsky, "Protiv idealizatsii deiatel'nosti Ivana IV" (Against idealiza-
tion of the activities of Ivan IV), *Voprosy Istorii*, No. 8 (1956), p. 128.

of peasant farming in the succeeding four years were the twin policy programs on the basis of which he carried through the process of total state regimentation of society. This was the period of the emergence of a full-blown, as distinguished from a merely embryonic, totalitarian state system. The policy programs called for more and more coercion and controls, including internal passports, massive regimentation of the labor force, more and more concentration camps, and police terror as an integral part of daily life. Expansion of controls and governmental functions called for more and more bureaucratic regulation; and this in turn further augmented the need for controls, including controls over the bureaucratic controllers, and so on in a vicious circle. Stalin, possibly with the image of Ivan the Terrible already in mind, christened the whole process the "building of socialism." Actually, it was the first great stage of Stalinization.

No sooner was the basic work accomplished (approximately in 1933) than Stalin turned his attention to the next and culminating step, which was to reconstitute the autocracy. This occupied about five years of time, from 1934 to 1939. That period witnessed the virtual extermination of the Bolshevik Party, carried out by Stalin in the name of Lenin and Bolshevism.

Every true totalitarianism is a one-man system and comes to power through the subversion of a pre-existing political regime. In the case of Hitler, the pre-existing regime was the Weimar Republic. In the case of Mussolini, it was the Italian constitutional monarchy. In those instances no one could doubt that a regime had been subverted. Stalin's case was exceptional, and therefore deceptive, because here the pre-existing regime was a ruthless party dictatorship, and the destruction of it was effected without any official admission or overly obvious sign that a continuity of political life was being broken. So authoritarian was the rule of the Bolshevik Party in Russia that it could be eliminated as a living political organism and replaced by the autocracy of Stalin without the world's quite realizing that something of real consequence had happened. But Stalin himself was at least subconsciously aware of what he had done, and showed it when, in 1952, he expunged the very word "Bolshevik" from the title of the party and the official vocabulary of the regime. He banned the use of the word "Bolshevik" in the Soviet Union, evidently feeling uncomfortable at the sight and sound of it. The word was revived immediately after he died.

This is a point of critical importance for the analysis both of

Soviet politics of the 1930's and 1940's and also of the post-Stalin period. We are accustomed to thinking in terms of a continuity of party rule in Soviet Russia from October 1917 to the present. Actually, however, after Stalin's blood purges of the middle 1930's there was no longer in any real sense a ruling *party*, just as there was no real ruling *class;* there was at most a privileged stratum of bureaucratic serving-men who lived well and wore medals but who were pure instrumentalities rather than holders or sharers of power. To call this stratum an "elite," as is sometimes done, is to invite misconception of the actual situation which had come to prevail under Stalin; it was only an ersatz elite.

The one-party system had given way to a one-person system, the ruling party to a ruling personage. Through the massacre of the bulk of the Bolshevik leadership and the exile of many thousands more, Stalin completed the transformation of the former ruling party into a transmission belt of autocracy, an administrative-bureaucratic mechanism totally submissive to his will. Only the *local* party bosses retained a semblance of actual authority. They became little dictators, ruling their localities at the pleasure of the big dictator in the Kremlin. And they had to watch out for the local head of the secret police, who was also working for Stalin.

Accordingly, although the Soviet Union continued to be a party-ruled state in Stalinist mythology, the former ruling party became in fact merely the first in importance of the mass organizations in the totalitarian system. This suppression of the party was especially accentuated after World War II. The post-Stalin regime has not openly admitted this. Its euphemistic formula is that the "cult of personality," as Stalin's absolute despotism is called, merely "diminished the role of the party.". . .

Thus, in the second major phase of Stalinization, which took place in the mid-1930's, Stalin created an absolute autocracy through the suppression of the Bolshevik Party. This meant, in effect, the liquidation of the Soviet ruling class.[3] Here again we must refer to Ivan the Terrible in order to elucidate the subjective rationale of Stalin's actions, the method in what might seem to be merely madness.

In directing the orgy of treason trials and executions of party cadres, Stalin imagined himself to be acting as Ivan had acted in asserting his absolutism against the ancient landed aristocracy, the

[3] The concept of the Party as the ruling class was introduced by Lenin, who said in August 1917: "Russia used to be ruled by 150,000 landlords. Why could not 240,000 Bolsheviks do the same job?"

Boyars, who were bloodily suppressed on charges of treason and sedition. He even used the pseudonym "Ivan Vasilyevich" (the first name and patronymic of Ivan the Terrible, the initials of which corresponded to those of his own first name and patronymic, Iosif Vissarionovich) in some secret inner correspondence of the purge period.[4] Later, in the conversation with the film director in 1947, he allowed himself to criticize Ivan on just one point. Ivan, he said, had made the mistake of failing to liquidate five remaining feudal families, had not carried through the suppression of the aristocracy to a finish; but for this omission, he suggested, there would have been no Time of Troubles in Russia after Ivan's death. "And then Iosif Vissarionovich added humorously that 'Here God interfered with Ivan': *Grozny* liquidates one feudal family, one Boyar line, and then for a whole year repents and prays forgiveness for the 'sin,' whereas what he should have done was to act still more decisively!" [5] Stalin, we see, not only took Ivan the Terrible as his political model; he conceived himself as the pupil who surpassed the master in the politics of the blood purge.

One further important point requires mention here. Ivan created an institution known as the *oprichnina,* which was an instrument for the liquidation of the Boyars and a mainstay in his adminstration of the state. The prerevolutionary Russian historian Kliuchevsky describes the *oprichnina* as an all-powerful security police. It was organized as a kind of state within the state. The *oprichniki* wore black and rode black horses; their special insignia consisted of a dog's head and a broom attached to the saddle. In the folk memory of the Russian people, the *oprichnina* lingers as a symbol of black crimes and terror, as does its chief, Ivan the Terrible. Stalin unquestionably modeled his NKVD quite consciously upon it. The Soviet security police, originally the terrorist weapon of the Bolshevik Party's dictatorship, became the weapon with which Stalin broke the back of the ruling party. Its functions expanded as its importance rose during the 1930's, until finally, under Stalin's direct guidance, it became a kind of state within the state, an *oprichnina* of Stalinist Russia, inspiring terror, practicing torture, watching over everything and everybody, carrying on the kidnaping of Soviet citizens as a matter of settled official policy. In the later Stalin years, the idealizing of Ivan the Terrible was extended to include the idealiz-

[4] Alexander Orlov, *The Secret History of Stalin's Crimes* (New York, 1953), p. 206.

[5] Dubrovsky, *loc. cit.*

ing of the *oprichnina*. Stalin inspired this, too. In the 1947 conversation in the Kremlin, "Iosif Vissarionovich noted also the progressive role of the *oprichnina*." [6]

If Stalin destroyed the Bolshevik Party as a political organism and ruling class, how, we may ask, did he take its place all by himself? What was the Stalin autocracy, considered as an institution? The basic political system has been described here as a complex, three-way, state-party-soviet structure of command and control of society. The autocracy, as Stalin reconstituted it, was a superstructure of command and control, superimposed upon this basic structure, making the Soviet system one single organization in the most literal sense of the word. Concerning the title and detailed operation of the actual organ of the autocracy, there is still some uncertainty. Some sources speak of a personal Stalin "secretariat." But according to a refugee account which seems authentic, the organ was something meshed in more closely with the actual machinery of rule.

It was the so-called "special sector" of the Central Committee apparatus, operated by and for Stalin along the lines of a personal secretariat. Through its own special representatives stationed at control positions, this organ operated the police system in accordance with Stalin's bidding. All his directives for trials and purges were funneled through it. All information was channeled into it. It had a foreign section through which Stalin conducted Soviet foreign policy, and so on. In short, the superstructure controlled and commanded the control and command apparatus at all key points. It was, as it were, a little gear box through which the entire massive machinery of Soviet rule over nearly 900,000,000 human beings on about one-third of the earth's surface was operated. By manipulating the levers in the control panel, Stalin could cause all kinds of things to happen. He could play politics as though on a piano, touching a key here and a chord there, with results as diverse as a blast in *Pravda* against Churchill, a purge in the Ukraine, a plan for a new power station on the Volga, a propaganda campaign about germ warfare, a re-evaluation of Einstein, or a government change in Bulgaria.

Naturally, this super-control system was not an efficient or even a rational instrument for governing a third of the earth. For various reasons, it failed to transmit upward much necessary information. Many needed decisions were not taken; many that were taken were not needed. The policy line—and there had to be a policy

[6] *Ibid.*

line on almost everything, even, for example, genetics—remained completely rigid until, at length, a particular key was touched, whereupon the shift was radical and instantaneous, and often quite demoralizing to the officialdom which had to implement it. The rigidity forced policy into maladjustment with ever-changing reality, and the radical shifts often widened rather than narrowed the gap. So the system, plainly, was not efficient. But it satisfied Stalin's craving for total control and command, and that, essentially, is why he built it up and perfected it, and also why he clung to it with compulsive tenacity despite all evidence that it was inefficient, sluggish, contrary to Soviet state interests, harmful to international communism, or anachronistic in an age of modern technology and swift events. It is not surprising that in his final years Stalin became a hidebound conservative in almost everything that had to do with the Soviet system: he wanted everything to stay just as it was—namely, under control.

One earlier incident testifies to the neurotic character of this need for total control. Khrushchev notes in the secret report Stalin's refusal, in 1941, to believe that Hitler intended to attack Russia—despite all warnings received—and also his great panic when the attack came. This behavior is explicable when we consider that the threat of attack, and later the attack itself, seemed to Stalin to jeopardize the entire control and command structure he had built up, which represented not only his life's work but, literally, his *life*—that is, his personality: he needed it in the same way that an addict needs his dope, and reacted to the threat of its downfall the way the addict would react to a threat to the dope supply—with panic. He said at the time, according to Khrushchev, "All that which Lenin created we have lost forever." [7] This, perhaps, was his way of saying: "All that *I* created is tottering, and I feel lost." Danger to Russia could not, as such, have caused these panic reactions in Stalin; but danger to his super-control system could. This helps to explain why nothing much could change in the Soviet Union until Stalin died, and also why various things immediately began to change when he *did* die. De-Stalinization did not start with Khrushchev's denunciation of Stalin in early 1956. The first and the essential act of de-Stalinization was the death of Stalin.

This analysis may help to bring into focus the much-discussed question of the relation between the Stalin autocracy and the Soviet order. It is often maintained that Stalin was a necessary

[7] See above, chapter 6, "Khrushchev 1956: The Cult Exposed"—Ed.

product of the "system." One objection to this argument is that it tends to regard the Soviet system as a static thing, born whole and intact out of the October Revolution. In reality, as the foregoing discussion indicates, there was a parallel and interactive evolution of the system and the autocracy. Thus, the Stalin phenomenon must be viewed as historical cause as well as historical effect. It is true that the pre-existing party dictatorship provided a highly favorable political milieu for Stalin's drive to absolute power. The Russian national tradition of centralized bureaucratic rule and passive popular acceptance of it also helped to smooth the path for Stalin. However, these objective circumstances did not make the rise of the Stalin autocracy inevitable; at most they made it a possible or probable tendency.

What converted the tendency into an historical reality was not the nature of Russia or the nature of Bolshevism: it was the nature of Stalin. That is, the nature of his personality was a factor of crucial importance in shaping the history of the Stalin period. Furthermore, once in existence, the autocracy became an autonomous historical force, reshaping its own political milieu, transforming the whole Soviet system into a mechanism for the projection of Stalin's power and personality. In this sense it may be said that the Stalinist political system was a product of Stalin. It is precisely the latter point that is overlooked, no doubt deliberately, by the Soviet view as voiced by Khrushchev in the secret report. That view treats the autocracy as a kind of regrettable excrescence on the otherwise healthy organism of the Soviet system, something which just grew and eventually caused all sorts of painful complications, now happily in the past. The elimination of the excrescence, it is held, restores the organism to its normal state of health. The official Soviet concept of de-Stalinization is founded on this false minimizing of the meaning of Stalinization. . . .

Would the Leninist party dictatorship have been transformed into a Stalinist-type totalitarian autocracy (*i.e.*, into Soviet fascism) if there had been no Stalin: if, say, J. Djugashvili had died in infancy? The answer to which the foregoing discussion points, and which the pages to follow will bring out more clearly, is: Perhaps, but not necessarily. For the pathological personality of Stalin was a critically important factor in the outcome. It could be argued, with this in mind, that if Stalin had never existed, some other equally and similarly pathological personality would have certainly been there to capitalize on conditions and shape events in like fashion. This is the position that an orthodox Marxist, for example, might take. But it is impossible to substantiate. How a Soviet Russia minus Stalin would have developed from the 1920's to the 1950's must remain, to some extent, an open question.

The period from the end of World War II in 1945 to Stalin's death in early 1953 forms the climax and concluding chapter in the development of Russian Stalinism. It was the period of Stalin's own greatest autocratic eminence in the affairs of Russia and of his personality's greatest impact upon the affairs of the external world. It might well be called the *Stalinshchina*—The Time of Stalin. The story of the currents and countercurrents of events inside Russia during those years is one of enormous inner complexity, and has not yet been fully and satisfactorily understood in the Western world. No serious effort at systematic analysis of it is possible in this brief over-all survey. However, a few salient points require mention.

One of the most important new developments of the postwar period was the externalizing of the Stalinization process. This had started with the Soviet occupation of the Baltic republics and eastern Poland in the period just prior to the war, but was interrupted by the Soviet-German hostilities. When the war ended, Stalin pushed ahead with a grandiose endeavor of Soviet empire-building, which carried Stalinization to most of Middle Europe and parts of Asia. Like the process inside Russia, Stalinization abroad proceeded through a series of consecutive stages. Now, however, the pattern having been laid down and the techniques learned and perfected, the agencies of Soviet power were able to compress the re-enactment into a very short span of years. The formation of the satellite empire meant the incorporation of the countries concerned into the Moscow command and control structure, their reduction to the status of Soviet "union republics" in all but name. Communist China, for various reasons, appears to have occupied a somewhat exceptional position in this picture, and Yugoslavia successfully rebelled against full-scale Stalinization. Otherwise the process was carried through consistently and to the fullest possible extent. . . .

From the internal Soviet point of view, the *Stalinshchina* meant, to begin with, "back to Stalinist normalcy." It is precisely for this reason that the year 1945 may be taken as the historical starting point of the internal political unrest which began to make itself evident on the surface of Russian life in the post-Stalin period and especially in the latter part of 1956. For the reimposition of Stalinism-as-usual was precisely what the Russian people as a whole did not want and did not expect in 1945. Popular sentiment was epitomized in the remark of a Russian army officer in Moscow on VE-Day: "Now it is time to live."

The term "reimposition" does not refer to the institutional structure, for that did not alter during the war years. However, the atmosphere of life in Russia did alter. In the face of the ordeal of invasion and the dread possibility that the Russian people would not support the defense effort, the Stalin regime relaxed the police controls somewhat, and particularly the police terror. Equally important, it took steps to encourage the belief among the people that the postwar period would be the beginning of a "new period" of growing internal abundance and freedom. . . .

These were some of the expectations of the Russians. *In effect, the people expected a beginning of de-Stalinization.* They expected to hear from Stalin at the war's end a speech similar to the one given by Malenkov in August 1953, when he announced a new course in which Russian energies would be invested, at least in part, in raising the Russian standard of life. Instead, when Stalin addressed them over the Soviet radio on February 9, 1946, he gave a lecture on the timeless virtues of the "Soviet method of industrialization," eulogized the collectivization of agriculture as its counterpart, sketched a vista of endless further five-year plans oriented toward heavy industry, signalized a new period of international tension, and extolled the Stalinist order as "superior to any non-Soviet social order" and "a form of organization of society which is perfectly stable and capable of enduring." [8]

This was Stalin's credo of conservatism in all that concerned the Stalinist structure of command and control. The system was to remain intact; nothing was to change. Thus were the popular hopes for a measure of postwar de-Stalinization dashed to pieces. "We were deceived!" echoes down the postwar years in the statements of Russians who escaped. They had fought and bled for a decent Russia. When it was all over, they received the *Stalinshchina*. Then and there, the prerequisites began to develop for an opposition movement from below.

However, this was not evident on the surface of events in the early postwar years. The popular attitude was not then notably rebellious; rebellion will appear only when desperation is ignited by a spark of hope. There was very little hope left in the people of Russia during the postwar years of Stalin's reign. What happened was that most people came to look upon the command and

[8] See above, chapter 1, "Stalinism As Usual"—ED.

control structure as an alien environment, something that had to be lived in perforce, but which was not a real home. . . . In all save a few special fields of national life, such as military production and heavy industry, signs of regress appeared. The system flourished; the society entered into decline.

No amount of propaganda and indoctrination could counteract this decline. Propaganda cannot either create or abolish feelings; at most, it can influence or channel feelings which already exist. This is one explanation for the steady growth of official anti-Semitism in the USSR after 1946. It was, in part, the regime's way of endeavoring to divert away from itself the popular resentment of a life lived in a maze of controls. But the very fact that this was resorted to shows how ineffective the regular lines of indoctrination were proving. The secret police, which reinstituted an atmosphere of continual pervasive terror in the postwar years, could not correct this situation. The terror could do no more than hold popular attitudes in check, combat outward manifestations here and there, enforce a sense of hopelessness. As we now know, hard-bitten Soviet officials in high places saw this phenomenon of estrangement and failure of response, and the damage that was resulting; and they realized that it was in the regime's own interests to try by other means than terror and propaganda to counteract it. But who would explain all this to Stalin? Who would tell him that the Russian people, or large elements of it, were inwardly emigrating? No one, of course. For Stalin doted on the image of himself as the darling of the people and the international working class, as the beloved "Leader and Teacher" of a prosperous nation and progressive empire. To call in question the condition of the realm would be to call in question this glorious, idealized self-image of Stalin, and woe betide the Soviet official—be he high or low—who dared do this.

What happened, then, was that, by mobilization of submissive artists and intellectuals, a servile officialdom made reality *seem* to do Stalin's bidding. That is, it created for Stalin a fantasy-picture of Soviet reality, transforming it in *Pravda* and films and novels into a beautiful world of happy workers and peasants and ever-advancing progress and productivity, marred only by a few "alien elements" which occasionally penetrated and caused something to go wrong. This was no Potemkin village; it was a Potemkin Russia, fabricated not out of wooden façades but out of words and pictures and symbols of all kinds—an image of a Russia which did not really exist, but was *supposed* to exist. It is not hard to see why

Stalin's death *had* to mean de-Stalinization. The Stalinist political order was a one-person system. The personality of Stalin was, by virtue of the intricate control mechanism described here, the focal force of Soviet politics, the sun around which the whole Soviet political universe revolved.

10

George F. Kennan
"Criminality Enthroned"[1]

It is hard to approach this subject [the personality, human and political, of Stalin himself] without speaking first about the great ethical conflict which wracked the Russian revolutionary movement of the nineteenth century. It was the conflict between the utopian humanitarianism of the ends and the harshness of the means. On the one hand, you had the unquestionable purity of the ideals by which these revolutionaries were driven; on the other, you had a terrible suspicion, growing gradually on the part of many of them into a belief, that the only path to the early realization of these ideals led through the perpetration of great cruelty against others. . . .

[This] meant that a few accepted the burden of guilt and unpleasantness in order that others might have the privilege of remaining guiltless. This was, in short, the classic Dostoyevskian dilemma.

I sometimes think the entire trend and fate of the Russian revolutionary movement can be explained in terms of the inability of the Russian intellectual class of the nineteenth century to cope with this dilemma. . . .

The Bolsheviki did not share this belief in personal terrorism. They rejected assassination as a normal means of political struggle. They rejected it not because they thought it was morally wrong but because they considered it was, as Lenin himself said,

[1] From George F. Kennan, *Russia and the West Under Lenin and Stalin* (Boston: Little, Brown and Company; London: Hutchinson & Co. Ltd., 1961), pp. 241-245, 247-258. Copyright © 1960, 1961 by James K. Hotchkiss, Trustee. Reprinted by permission of the author, Atlantic—Little, Brown & Co. and The Hutchinson Publishing Group. (Pagination from English edition.)

"inopportune and inexpedient." [2] But their rejection of individual terrorism did not in any sense signify a repudiation of violence. Lenin, scarred no doubt by his brother's death on a Tsarist gallows, wholly accepted the need for violence in the overthrow of the power of the propertied classes. . . .

One of the first points at which Lenin had occasion to authorize the resort to violence for Party purposes was in the use of brutal and criminal methods as a means of procuring funds for the support of Party activity. It is revealing and symbolic that it should have been precisely at this point, and in this connection, that Stalin came in. . . . There were those in the Party who wished to meet the financial deficits by resorting to methods which, while they were called by more polite names within the Party, we would most easily recognize as those of blackmail. . . .

The leadership of the Social-Democratic Party, in the period before the final split, officially opposed methods of violence as fundraising devices. . . . Lenin, while outwardly accepting the Party's position, had no objection in practice to seeing the coffers of his own faction replenished by these dubious devices, wherever this could be quietly and inconspicuously done. There is no question but that he tolerated and encouraged actions of this sort, particularly on the part of the Caucasian comrades, during the difficult years from 1906 to 1912. And all signs indicate that it was in this dim realm where revolutionary politics merged with common criminality—in this world of fierce racial and personal hatreds, of intrigues and plots, daggers and murders, of fantastic vows and equally fantastic betrayals—that Stalin had his origins as a revolutionist.

Let us recall to mind, at this point, the duality that marked the Bolshevik faction as a whole. The Bolsheviki, as a political entity, embraced two quite disparate wings. Abroad, in the emigration, there was what I might call—if I may use a sort of Freudian and sociological term—the cosmopolitan-legitimate wing of the party: *cosmopolitan,* because it was composed of people who were citizens, not exactly of the world, but at least of the world socialist movement . . . and *legitimate,* in the sense that these people felt themselves to be a part of something which had a great and deep sort of legitimacy, which was founded in the very respectability of Marxism as a science. These people lived and moved in the world of European intellectual socialism. They acquired its manners and

[2] Bertram D. Wolfe, *Three Who Made a Revolution: A Biographic History* (New York, the Dial Press, 1948), p. 89.

affectations. In its approval they sought the rewards of their effort. They acknowledged a respect, if not for the opinions of all mankind, then at least for those of a considerable segment of it. They professed to hate the "bourgeoisie" as a class; but in their habits and personal outlooks there was a good deal of bourgeois propriety and self-respect—sometimes even pretension.

Opposed to this wing of the Party was that which remained in Russia and functioned, perforce, in the underground. This wing I should like to call the criminal-defiant one: *criminal,* because an outstanding feature of its psychology was the fact that it was outside the law in relation to its own environment; *defiant,* because it had the typical psychology of the hardened and committed outlaw, of the person who has burned his bridges, who regards his breach with society as final and irreparable, who has accepted society as an enemy whether or not society has accepted him in the same way, and who seeks vindication for his rebellion in the very glamour of his struggle against society, in the danger he undergoes, in the valor he exhibits in thus exposing himself to this danger, in the fear and respect he engenders in his own criminal circle by the extremity of his despair, his resolve, and his lack of scruple. These underground Bolsheviki were the original bad boys—unregenerate and incorrigible. And nowhere, let us note, were these qualities more pronounced, nowhere do they provide more of a contrast to the mild intellectual sincerity of the exiled wing of the Party, than in the seething, savage underworld of the Transcaucasus. . . .

Thirteen years were to elapse between the time of Stalin's expulsion from the seminary and his recruitment, in 1912, into the senior echelons of the Bolshevik Party, for work outside his native Caucasus. [The author goes on to discuss the paucity of official information on this period of Stalin's career—ED.]

Three hypotheses have been advanced to explain this state of affairs. One is that Stalin was concerned to conceal his obscurity in the Party at that time. Another is that he was so closely connected with certain of the criminal fund-raising activities of the Party that an exposure of his doings in those years would not fit well with the carefully cultivated image of the later great statesman. The third hypothesis is that he was an ordinary police informer, or at least that his relations with the police were such that they would be difficult to explain. My own feeling is that all three of these hypotheses may have had some truth in them. . . .

There is a considerable body of evidence . . . which suggests that Stalin even in those early years was known to his comrades in the Caucasus as a trouble-maker—a person with a fondness for stirring up resentments and suspicions among others, for provoking others into quarrels and acts of violence, and in this way getting his revenge on people who had in some way offended him or stood in his path.

In 1912, for reasons as yet unclarified,[3] Stalin was suddenly lifted out of his obscurity and made a member of the Central Committee of what was now the Bolshevik Party. . . .

When in 1917—having been liberated by the first Russian Revolution—Stalin returned to Petrograd and resumed activity as a senior official of the Party, he had still had relatively little contact with that brilliant cosmopolitan-legitimate wing of the party to which I referred a few moments ago. His previous experience in the central offices of the Party outside the Caucasus had been very brief, and related to a period already four or five years in the past. To the people around him—the Trotskys, the Zinovievs, the Kamenevs, the Bukharins—Stalin was at that time almost an unknown quantity. . . . These intellectuals, who made up the great majority of Lenin's entourage, were men far better educated than Stalin, more literate, more eloquent, more prominent in the revolutionary movement. They were the great dramatic figures of the Revolution. Stalin was only a colorless drone in the Party's administrative offices. He didn't even speak proper Russian—at least he didn't speak it with a proper accent—to say nothing of the foreign tongues in which so many of the others were proficient. He was without originality in the intellectual and literary sense. He had no personal charm,[4] no oratorical gifts.

Compare these facts, now, with what we know today to have been Stalin's personal nature. This was a man dominated, as his whole subsequent record of thirty years in the public eye demonstrates, by an insatiable vanity and love of power, coupled with the keenest sort of sense of his own inferiority and a burning jealousy for qualities in others which he did not possess. He had certain well-known characteristics of the Caucasian mountain race to which his father is said to have belonged—an inordinate touchiness, an endless vindictiveness, an inability ever to forget an insult or a slight, but great patience and power of dissimulation in

---

[3] See, however, Deutscher, *Stalin*, pp. 109-12—ED.

[4] But cf., for instance, chapter 4 "Davies: 'Kindly and Wise' "—ED.

selecting and preparing the moment to settle the score. He is said once to have observed that there was nothing sweeter in life than to bide the proper moment for revenge, to insert the knife, to turn it around, and to go home for a good night's sleep. At the same time, let us note, he was a man with the most extraordinary talent for political tactics and intrigue, a consummate actor, a dissimulator of genius, a master not only of timing but of what Boris Nikolayevsky has called the art of "dosage"—of doing things gradually, of measuring out what the traffic would bear on any given occasion. He was a master, in particular, of the art of playing people and forces off against each other, for his own benefit. It was not he, actually, who inserted the knife; he had ways of getting others to do it for him. He merely looked on with benign detachment, sometimes even with grief and indignation. . . .

If we picture to ourselves a man of this temperament, and then bear in mind the situation in which, as we have just seen, he found himself placed, in the initial period following the Revolution, it will not be difficult to see why he should have reacted in ways that were bound to affect his conduct as the head of the Soviet state. He was, first of all, extremely sensitive to the loneliness of his position vis-à-vis other leaders of the Party. He had not shared their background and their attainments. This world of international socialism . . . this was a world to which Stalin did not belong, and knew he did not belong. Its values were not his values. Of its own inclination, it would, he knew, never respect or support him. He could win leadership in this world only by outwitting it, by intimidating it, by exploiting its inner contradictions, and by enlisting against it the forces of the Communist underground movement in Russia and of the young recruits who flowed into the Party after the Revolution on the flood tide of its political success. These latter elements, like himself, had no intimacy with the older Party intellectuals. To all of them, the myths and memories surrounding the Party's former life in exile—the struggles, the feuds, the arguments, and the intrigues of Geneva and Vienna and Krakow —were remote and unreal, already passing into history. Stalin, in short, exploited against the previously exiled wing of the Party both that portion of the old Party which had served in Russia and the many postrevolutionary fair-weather adherents to whom the heroic days of the struggle in exile would never be more than a legend.

In those years immediately after the Revolution the former exiles still constituted, in effect, the political and ideological leadership of the Party. Stalin had to exercise the utmost prudence in opposing them. If he attacked them prematurely or rashly they . . . would isolate him. They would alienate from him the whole great European socialist movement, to which they had personal access and over which they had influence—the movement of which Russian Communism originally conceived itself a part, in which it aspired to leadership, from the umbilical cord of which it was still too weak to be severed, and without which the Revolution in Russia made no ideological sense.

Stalin was well aware of this danger. It made a profound impression on him. He could never forget it, in later years. Even after his ascendancy in Russia had become virtually unchallenged, the pretense had always to be maintained that at least a large portion—the virtuous and correct portion—of the European socialist movement was enthusiastically in accord with his regime in Russia, and looked to it with admiration and fidelity. This pretense was the revelation of his greatest anxiety. . . . He seems never to have lost the fear that if his rivals ever succeeded in enlisting against him the moral force of socialist opinion *outside* Russia, his rule could be shaken and he could be lost.

Out of this nightmare flowed some of the well-known aspects of his motivation as a statesman. From this, there came his aversion to really spontaneous and successful revolutions by any of the foreign communist parties. He recognized clearly that so long as these parties remained struggling opposition groups, caught in the network of their own semi-criminal defiance of established authority within *their* respective countries, they would have a dependence on Soviet support—a dependence which he, as head of the Soviet state, could exploit in order to keep them under control. Their condition would be similar to his previous condition in the Caucasus; he would know how to deal with them. If on the other hand they were actually to come into power and to achieve the ability to dispose, as he was now able to dispose, over the resources of a great country, this dependence would be lost. From this came his insistence on rigid disciplinary control of the foreign communist parties, even at the expense of their morale, of their popular appeal, and of their prospects for coming into power. So long as he could control in this way at least a portion of the foreign communist and socialist movements, he could be sure of preventing the growth, within that portion, of that defiant and hostile unity, and particularly of that alliance between it and his rivals at home, which remained to his dying day the greatest of his fears.

It was, of course, not only the world of foreign socialism and communism which Stalin feared and with which he had to contend. There was also the bourgeois world—the so-called "capitalist encirclement." This, too, could be a mortal danger to him, if its hostility ever again took the form—as it had in 1917 and 1918—of war and military intervention.

Now, it is important to note that during the decades of Stalin's rule this danger of military hostility against the Soviet Union by capitalist countries was sometimes real and sometimes not real. . . . Yet these fluctuations in the degree of external danger found no reflection in the interpretation of world realities which Stalin put forward for internal consumption. He generally portrayed Russia to his followers as threatened, whether this was true at the moment, or whether it was untrue. Not only this, but he took pains to confuse as far as possible in the public mind the two dangers here involved —the danger of opposition to himself by foreign socialists and communists, and the danger of capitalist intervention.

Why did he do this? He did it because the one fear was respectable, the other was not. One concerned the fortunes of the movement and the country; the other concerned his personal position. He wanted to hide his fear of foreign socialism and communism, and to disguise the measures he took to defend himself against this danger, behind an apparent concern for the security of the Soviet Union. It was to this end that he constantly and systematically exaggerated the possibility of hostile military intervention against the Soviet state. It was to this end that he labored so assiduously to identify communist and socialist rivals with hostile bourgeois forces —calling the German Social-Democrats "Social-Fascists," confusing Trotsky with Hitler in the nightmarish inventions of the purge trials, forcing his communist victims with monotonous regularity, over the years, to confess to being the agents of foreign interventionists, as a last act of expiation and self-humiliation before being shot.

But do not be deceived as to which of these apprehensions—the admitted one or the concealed one, the apprehension of danger to his personal position or that of danger to the Soviet state—was the greatest. Trotsky, and all that Trotsky represented, was Stalin's real fear; Hitler was largely his excuse for fear. This is why his measures of defense against Hitler were singularly unreal and ineffective. He was prepared for the pretense, the artificial bugbear, of capitalist intervention, but not for its reality. On the one occasion, after Lenin's death, when this specter took on flesh and blood and became a reality—when the German troops, that is, stormed into Russia in 1941—this man, who had cried "Wolf" so long and insistently, became for the first time quite paralyzed and helpless, lost his nerve, and had to be bailed out by the men around him.

To say these things is not to imply that Stalin had no real policy towards the bourgeois world or no real interest in Russia's relations with it. He was a man of extraordinarily wide and sensitive understanding of political issues and events, even on the world scale. He rarely missed a trick. He recognized perfectly clearly the forces of the non-Communist world. He accepted them, in the traditional Soviet Communist manner, as hostile forces, viewed them without sympathy or pity, and dealt with them no less coldbloodedly than he did with the component forces of the world communist movement.

But here, too, his fundamental motive was the protection of his own personal position. Sometimes the interests of his personal position were identical with those of the Soviet state in its rivalry with the bourgeois world. Sometimes, . . . they were not. . . .

The policies to which this preoccupation led were, in essence, very simple. From the bourgeois world, as from his political entourage in the world of communism, Stalin wanted only one thing: weakness. This was not at all identical with revolution. Unless other states were very small, and contiguous to Russia's borders, so that there were good prospects for controlling them by the same concealed police methods he employed in Russia, Stalin did not want other states to be communist. He was concerned only that they should be weak, or that they should at least expend their strength not against him and his regime but against each other. For this reason his favored strategy was a simple one. It could be summed up in the single phrase "divide and rule." It consisted in the instinctive effort—the same to which he was so addicted in personal life—to divide his opponents, to provoke them to hostile action against each other, to cause them to waste *their* strength in this way, while he conserved *his.*

This strategy was applied, without distinction, towards all external forces: communist, socialist, and capitalist alike. . . .

Little effort was ever made on Stalin's part to create new issues. He was content to make the most of those apples of discord with which Nature had so liberally endowed the human community. His agents were taught to search for these existing differences and to exploit them to the limit. It was largely a matter of indifference to Stalin *what* others fought with each other about; the main thing was that they should fight. He was no doctrinaire ideologist. He knew that theoretical ideas meant things to other people; no one, in fact, was more sensitive than he to the understanding of *what* it was that they meant, or more skillful in exploiting the political-emotional impulses to which ideas gave rise. But he did not share these impulses. He only understood them. To him, ideas meant nothing in their own right. They had meaning only as the determinants of action—as the symbols and rationalizations of political attitudes. He could therefore be—and was—quite catholic in his use of divisive and disruptive tactics. Whatever was not *his* could, on principle, well be weakened. The only thing you had to watch was that the weakening of one side did not proceed so fast that the other had a bloodless triumph. No force must be annihilated before it had done its own work of destruction.

And these principles went for domestic as well as for foreign policy. Stalin, in fact, did not really recognize a difference. To him, the border between foreign and domestic affairs was an artificial one. He was, in his own eyes, the enemy of all the world. The Russian people and the Russian Communist Party were as much his adversaries as were the German Trotskyites or the Yugoslav renegades or the world of capitalism. Just as the Party itself remained, down to World War II, officially and formally a conspiratorial organization within Russia, working within and against the very popular masses which it was supposed to represent, so Stalin's personal secretariat remained a conspiracy within and against the Party as a whole.

But there was a difference. Outside Russia, Stalin's physical power was extremely limited. . . . In Russia, these inhibitions did not exist. And it was here that his whole unconscionable ambition and ruthlessness found their expression. We know pretty well today what at one time we could only suspect: that this was a man of incredible criminality, of a criminality effectively without limits; a man apparently foreign to the very experience of love, without pity or mercy; a man in whose entourage no one was ever safe; a man whose hand was set against all that could not be useful to him at the moment; a man who was most dangerous of all to those who were his closest collaborators in crime, because he liked to be the sole custodian of his own secrets, and disliked to share his memories or his responsibility with others who, being still alive, had tongues and consciences and might be susceptible to the human weaknesses of remorse or indiscretion.

As the outlines of Stalin's personal actions begin to emerge, through the fog of confusion and irrelevance with which he loved to surround them during his lifetime, we are confronted with a record beside which the wildest murder mystery seems banal. I cannot attempt to list the man's crimes. Trotsky seriously charged that Stalin poisoned Lenin. He certainly wished to give him poison. He evidently either killed his young wife in 1932, or drove her to suicide in his presence. There is every probability, in the light of evidence now available, that it was Stalin himself who inspired the murder of his Number Two in the Party, S. M. Kirov, in 1934. How many others there were among the senior members of Stalin's intimate entourage who, while ostensibly in good standing, died as a result of Stalin's malignant ministrations, we can only guess. There are at least half a dozen—including the writer Maxim Gorky and such close Party comrades as Sergo Ordzhonikidze and A. A. Zhdanov—of whom this seems probable. That the man who split Trotsky's skull with an ax in Mexico City in 1940 did so at Stalin's instigation is beyond question. By way of response, apparently, to what seems to have been some opposition to his purposes on the part of the seventeenth Party Congress in 1934, Stalin killed, in the ensuing purges of 1936 to 1938, 1108 out of a total of 1966 of the members of the Congress. Of the Central Committee elected at that Congress and still officially in office, he killed 98 out of 139—a clear majority, that is, of the body from which ostensibly he drew his authority. These deaths were only a fraction, numerically, of those which resulted from the purges of those years. Most of the victims were high officials of the Party, the army, or the Soviet government apparatus.

All this is aside from the stupendous brutalities which Stalin perpetrated against the common people: notably in the process of collectivization, and also in some of his wartime measures. The number of victims here—the number, that is, of those who actually lost their lives—runs into the millions. But this is not to mention the broken homes, the twisted childhoods, and the millions of people who were half-killed: who survived these ordeals only to linger on in misery, with broken health and broken hearts.

Plainly, such excesses reached far beyond what was required for the protection of one man's personal position. In part, they seem to have been the product of real mental disturbance. But even to the extent they represented rational action from the standpoint of Stalin's personal interests, they coincided only in a limited area with the real needs, external and internal, of the country at the head of which he stood. Much of what Stalin did was irrelevant to the needs of Russia. Another part was clearly in conflict with those needs. In some ways, certainly, Russia benefited from Stalin's indisputable qualities of greatness. But in other respects there was a price to be paid for his leadership, externally as well as internally —a price which is still being paid, not just by Russia but by the world at large. . . .

It remains only to mention the contrast between Stalin, as a statesman, and the man he succeeded in the position of supreme power in Russia. The differences are not easy ones to identify, for in many instances they were only ones of degree and of motive. Lenin, too, was a master of internal Party intrigue. He, too, was capable of ruthless cruelty. He, too, could be unpitying in the elimination of people who seriously disagreed with him or seemed to him to stand in the path of the best interests of the Party. No less than Stalin, Lenin adopted an attitude of implacable hostility toward the Western world; and so long as the Western powers were stronger than Russia, which was the case throughout his lifetime, he, too, based his policies on the hope of dividing them one from another and playing them off against one another.

But behind all this there were very significant differences. Lenin was a man with no sense of inferiority. . . . He was spared that whole great burden of personal insecurity which rested so heavily on Stalin. He never had to doubt his hold on the respect and admiration of his colleagues. He could rule them through the love they bore him, whereas Stalin was obliged to rule them through their fears. This enabled Lenin to run the movement squarely on the basis of what he conceived to be *its* needs, without bothering about his own. And since the intellectual inventory of the Party was largely of his own creation, he was relieved of that ignominious need which Stalin constantly experienced for buttressing his political views by references to someone else's gospel. Having fashioned Leninism to his own heart's desire out of the raw materials of Marx's legacy, Lenin had no fear of adapting it and adjusting it as the situation required. For this reason, his mind remained open throughout his life—open, at least, to argument and suggestion from those who shared his belief in the basic justification of the second Russian Revolution of 1917. These people could come to him and talk to him, and could find their thoughts not only accepted in the spirit they were offered but responded to by a critical intelligence second to none in the history of the socialist movement. They did not have to feel, as they later did under Stalin, that deep, dangerous, ulterior meanings might be read into anything they said, and that an innocent suggestion might prove their personal undoing. . . .

All this rendered even more difficult the problem which Soviet power in Russia presented for the outside world. In Lenin's day the differences were deep, and seemingly irreconcilable; but it was possible, if one had the wit and the brutality to fall in with the tone of Soviet discussion, to talk about them with the Soviet leaders, and to obtain at least some clarification as to where things stood. In Stalin's day, this was no longer possible. He had no taste for even that brutal, sardonic, uncompromising frankness with which Lenin faced the representative of the class enemy. His addiction to the arts of deception was too profound to be separable from his intellectual calculations. Unlike Lenin, who could view objective reality as something apart from himself, Stalin was able to see the world only through the prism of his own ambitions and his own fears. The foreigner who talked to Stalin could never be sure just what he was dealing with—whether it was the interests of the movement or the interests of Stalin which stood in his path. Against this background, even the nature of the antagonism between the two worlds tended to become blurred and ambiguous. Not until the personality of Khrushchev replaced that of Stalin at the pinnacle of authority in the Soviet regime did it again become possible, as it had been in Lenin's time, to have at least a clear-cut dialogue about the differences that divided the Russian Communist world from its non-Communist environment.

Afterword.
Stalin Known and Unknown

We have not set out in this book to tell the reader what to think about Stalin. Our object has been to assist him in making his own observations, to introduce him to the most influential and interesting general evaluations of Stalin, and to encourage him to test the one against the other. It would therefore be a betrayal of our purpose to present him now with a "summary" of the materials we have assembled or a neat set of "conclusions." Nonetheless, a few final remarks may help place our subject in perspective, without, we trust, unduly obtruding upon the reader's own evaluative processes.

On one point there appears to be near unanimity among our authors: the high level of Stalin's political skills, as these were defined in our introduction. This applies even to writers like Trotsky, whose values impel him to set minor store by such skills, or to Kennan, who regards the way Stalin *employed* these skills as utterly criminal.

Beyond this, opinion diverges sharply. What some see as patience, others see as deviousness; what some see as peasant wisdom, others see as craftiness; what some see as natural charm and sincerity, others see as brilliant playacting; what some see as firmness and decisiveness, others see as ruthlessness; what some see as devotion to the Revolution, others see as obsession with his own power.

And what of Stalin the thinker? Was he a talented interpreter of Leninism? Did he make significant contributions of his own to Marxist-Leninist theory? A low estimate of Stalin's theoretical grasp and originality is implicit in most recent writing on Stalin, both in Russia and the West. In our view Professor McNeal has performed a valuable service in reopening this question, which must assume major importance for Stalin's future biographers.

Further, how much did Stalin personally "determine" his own political actions, the shape assumed by the Soviet system, and Soviet relations with the outside world, and how much did he simply figure as the product or the instrument of social, economic, or historical forces? Our answer to this question must depend in large

177

part on our general views on the motive forces and mechanics of human history, although questions of fact inevitably become important when we attempt to argue it out. Any effort to arrange our authors along a determinism scale, moreover (say: Trotsky-Carr-Deutscher-Souvarine-Kennan-McNeal-Tucker), will be bedevilled by the inconsistencies of which some of these authors are themselves guilty, and by the different vantage points from which they have approached the facts. In this book we could do no more than introduce this problem; in the bibliographical note there are suggestions as to how the reader might follow it up.

Finally, let us recall the enormous gaps in our knowledge of the facts. How little we know about Stalin's childhood and youth, the details of his revolutionary career, his personal life after the revolution, or the inside political history of the Stalin era! Since 1953 Soviet political leaders, scholars, and memoirists have divulged a few tantalizing scraps of information. It is ultimately in the same direction that we must look for a remedy for our ignorance. Despite the high incidence of violent death among Stalin's close collaborators, there still survive men and women who were in close touch with him at the various stages of his political career. In all probability there are also members of his personal staff, servants, and relatives, as well as old men and women who remember him as a boy in Gori, or at the Tiflis Seminary. Is it too much to hope that a careful and thorough exploration of these sources will be undertaken before it is too late? As Nikita Khrushchev said at the Soviet Twenty-second Congress in 1961, speaking of the events of the Stalin era: "Time will pass and we will die, for we are all mortal, but so long as we can work we can and must clarify a great deal and tell the truth to the party and the people. It is our obligation to do everything to ensure that the truth is established now, since the more time passes after these events, the harder it will be to reconstruct the truth." [1] If the Soviet regime proves to possess a sufficient maturity and sense of responsibility toward history to ensure that all available facts about Stalin are gathered and reported in honest and scholarly fashion, while there is still time, few things will do its image more good, both among its own thinking citizens, and among the people of the world.

[1] *XXII s"ezd KPSS. Stenograficheskii otchët* (Moscow, 1962), II, 584.

Bibliographical Note

This note confines itself to some of the principal books relating to Stalin available in English. Students will also find it useful to consult Francis Randall's article "Books on Stalin," *Problems of Communism,* XII: 2 (March-April 1963).

The most useful volume of Stalin's own writings is J. Stalin, *Problems of Leninism* (Moscow, 1945 and other editions). The thirteen volumes so far published of Stalin's *Works* (English ed., Moscow, 1952-55) purport to cover the period to 1934, but there are numerous omissions (see Robert H. McNeal, "A Preface to Stalin's *Sochineniia, Survey: A Journal of Soviet and East European Affairs,* No. 49, October 1963). Another useful collection is Joseph Stalin, *Marxism and the National and Colonial Question* (London, n.d.). A number of Stalin's speeches and articles are available in various pamphlet editions and collections of Party Congress materials: his few postwar writings ("Marxism and Questions of Linguistics," 1946 and 1950 "electoral" speeches, "Economic Problems of Socialism in the U.S.S.R.," Speech at the Nineteenth Congress of the C.P.S.U.) exist only in this form. *Stalin's Kampf: Joseph Stalin's Credo Written By Himself,* edited by M. R. Werner (London, 1940), is an attempt to present various writings and statements of Stalin in the form of a comprehensive statement of his world-view. For a typical example of official exegesis, see A. Y. Vyshinsky, *The Teachings of Lenin and Stalin on the Proletarian Revolution and the State* (London, 1948). The best scholarly analysis of Stalin's thought is to be found in Gustav A. Wetter, *Dialectical Materialism* (New York, 1959; London, 1958) and Robert C. Tucker, *The Soviet Political Mind* (New York and London, 1963).

There are a number of general histories, histories of the Soviet Communist Party, and studies of the Soviet political system which are useful for placing Stalin in context. In the first category, see especially Donald W. Treadgold, *Twentieth Century Russia* (Chicago, 1959), Georg Von Rauch, *A History of Soviet Russia* (New York, 1957), and E. H. Carr's, *A History of Soviet Russia* of which six volumes, going up to 1926, have so far appeared (New York and London, 1950-   ). In the second category, see Leonard Schapiro, *The*

Communist Party of the Soviet Union (New York, 1960) and *The Origin of the Communist Autocracy* (Cambridge, Mass., and London, 1955), John A. Armstrong, *The Politics of Totalitarianism* (New York, 1961), John S. Reshetar, *A Concise History of the Soviet Communist Party* (New York, 1960), and Robert V. Daniels, *The Conscience of the Revolution: Communist Opposition in Soviet Russia* (Cambridge, Mass., and London, 1960). In the third category the most useful work is Merle Fainsod, *How Russia is Ruled* (2nd ed., Cambridge, Mass., 1963). On the internal politics of the Stalin era, see Robert Conquest, *Power and Policy in the U.S.S.R.* (New York and London, 1961), and on the external politics, George F. Kennan, *Russia and the West Under Lenin and Stalin* (Boston and London, 1961), and Marshall D. Shulman, *Stalin's Foreign Policy Reappraised* (Cambridge, Mass., 1963).

The principal official biographies of Stalin are E. Yaroslavsky, *Landmarks in the Life of Stalin* (London, 1942), and *Joseph Stalin: A Short Biography* (2nd ed., Moscow, 1947). The most useful collection of documents illustrating Communist reassessment of Stalin to 1956 is Columbia University Russian Institute, *The Anti-Stalin Campaign and International Communism* (New York, 1956). See also *On the Question of Stalin* (Peking, 1963). For a sympathetic account by a Western Communist, see Henri Barbusse, *Stalin, A New World Seen Through One Man* (New York and London, 1935). The "classical" biographies are Boris Souvarine, *Stalin, A Critical Survey of Bolshevism* (New York, 1939), Leon Trotsky, *Stalin, An Appraisal of the Man and His Influence* (New York, 1941; London, 1947), and Isaac Deutscher, *Stalin: A Political Biography* (New York and London, 1949). All early Western biographies are grossly overdrawn. The most reliable is Isaac Don Levine, *Stalin* (New York, 1931). See also Essad-Bey, *Stalin, the Career of a Fanatic* (New York, 1932), and Emil Ludwig, "Stalin, the Russian Autocrat," in his *Leaders of Europe* (London, 1934). Many attempts at popular biographies were distorted by the prevailing political attitudes, either unfavorably to Stalin as in the case of Eugene Lyons, *Stalin: Czar of All the Russias* (New York, 1940), and Frank Owen, *The Three Dictators: Mussolini, Stalin, Hitler* (London, 1940), or favorably as in the case of David M. Cole, *Joseph Stalin: Man of Steel* (London, 1942), Emil Ludwig, *Stalin* (New York, 1942), and J. T. Murphy, *Stalin, 1879-1944* (London, 1945). Of more permanent value are Bertram D. Wolfe, *Three Who Made a Revolution: A Biographical History* (New York, 1948), Max Nomad, *The Hierarch: Joseph Stalin, the*

Great Disciple (Boston, 1939), Nikolaus Basseches, *Stalin* (New York, 1952), and Louis Fischer, *The Life and Death of Stalin* (New York, 1952). Yves Delbars, *The Real Stalin* (London, 1953), aims at objectivity but suffers sadly from inaccuracy and naïveté of judgment.

Little of the early memoir material on Stalin's life and career is available in English. Though none of it is free from distortions of hindsight, prejudice, or sensationalism, some, such as the works of Iremashvili and Bajanov, is of considerable interest to the historian. Useful references to and assessments of these sources are contained in Trotsky's and Deutscher's biographies. Of later reminiscences, the most valuable and reliable are Walter Krivitsky, *I Was Stalin's Agent* (New York, 1945), and Alexander Barmine, *One Who Survived* (New York, 1945). Alexander Uralov's *The Reign of Stalin* (London, 1953) has the advantage of the author's first-hand experience as a middle-level Party official before World War II, but frequently lapses from accuracy. Of outstanding importance is Milovan Djilas, *Conversations with Stalin* (New York, 1962).

In addition to those works by foreign statesmen giving impressions or evaluations of Stalin, which we have excerpted in chapter 4, the following will also repay examination: Wendell L. Wilkie, *One World* (New York, London, etc., 1943), Harry S. Truman, *Memoirs,* esp. Vol. I (New York, 1955), Robert Sherwood, *Roosevelt and Hopkins: An Intimate History* (New York, 1948), and *The Memoirs of Cordell Hull,* esp. Vol. II (New York and London, 1948). Of the innumerable books on Stalin's Russia by Western journalists, four deserve specific mention: Louis Fischer, *Men and Politics* (New York, 1941), Alexander Werth, *The Year of Stalingrad* (New York, 1947), Walter Duranty, *Stalin & Co: The Politburo: The Men Who Run Russia* (New York, 1949), and Harrison E. Salisbury, *American In Russia* (New York, 1955).

Much of importance for evaluating Stalin's historical role is contained in specialized works, largely in learned journals, in such fields as political sociology, social psychology, economic history, and international affairs. The student desiring to broach this vast literature is recommended to start with Carl J. Friedrich and Zbigniew K. Brzezinski, *Totalitarian Dictatorship and Autocracy* (Cambridge, Mass., 1956), Hannah Arendt, *The Origins of Totalitarianism* (New York and London, 1951; English ed. entitled *The Burden of Our Time*), Alexander Dallin, *Soviet Conduct in World Affairs* (New York, 1960), Alexander Erlich, *The Soviet Industrialization Debate 1924-1928* (Cambridge, Mass., 1960), and Alec Nove, *Economic Ra-*

tionality and Soviet Politics; or, Was Stalin Really Necessary? (New York and London, 1964; English ed. entitled *Was Stalin Really Necessary? Some Problems of Soviet Political Economy*). A useful collection of materials oriented toward this problem is Robert V. Daniels, ed., *The Stalin Revolution* (Boston, 1965).